Charles L. Jones.

1973.

In review, ment... other reviews.

Reminder

Need to produce handouts with mobility tables, formulae, and algorithm-instructions for
(a) 2nd Ordinary Sociology
(b) Social Mobility. Kource Jan. Hong.

Have xerox of the translation of Boudon's 'Utopia' paper put in RR

# MATHEMATICAL STRUCTURES OF SOCIAL MOBILITY

# Progress in
# Mathematical Social Sciences

# MATHEMATICAL STRUCTURES OF SOCIAL MOBILITY

by

## RAYMOND BOUDON

Groupe d'Etude des Méthodes de l'Analyse Sociologique,
Université René Descartes, Paris, France

 Elsevier Scientific Publishing Company

Amsterdam · London · New York 1973

*For the U.S.A. and Canada:*

JOSSEY-BASS INC. PUBLISHERS

615 MONTGOMERY STREET

SAN FRANCISCO, CALIF. 94111


*For all other areas:*

ELSEVIER SCIENTIFIC PUBLISHING COMPANY

335 JAN VAN GALENSTRAAT

P.O. BOX 211, AMSTERDAM, THE NETHERLANDS


With 5 illustrations and 26 tables

Library of Congress Card Number: 73-77072

ISBN 0-444-41134-8

Printed in The Netherlands

# Progress in Mathematical Social Sciences

# Other books included in this series

**Lee M. Wiggins**
Panel Analysis — Latent Probability Models for Attitude and
Behavior Processes

**J.K. Lindsey**
Inferences from Sociological Survey Data — a Unified Approach

**Abram DeSwaan**
Coalition Theories and Cabinet Formations — a Study of Formal
Theories of Coalition Formation Applied to Nine European
Parliaments after 1918

*find Taylor ?
Taylor !    look on
aggregate data
analyse.*

# Acknowledgments

This monograph is a by-product of the author's work on social mobility (*L'inegalite des chances*, Paris, A. Colin, to be published). When I started working in this field, I felt it necessary to survey the mathematical literature dealing with social mobility with a sociologist's eye. I organized seminars on the subject and benefited much from the interest, remarks and personal work of several students: M. Bedart, M. Cherkaoui, M. El Houri, J. Lindsey and C. Paradeise were particularly helpful.

I am especially grateful to colleagues who agreed to read the manuscript and who sent me their useful suggestions and comments: D. Bartholomew, N. Henry, D. McFarland, J. Matras; to D. Handley who revised the whole text, and to J. Lindsey who applied his statistical competence to the material dealt with in this monograph. At an earlier stage, I also benefited very much from E. Bourco's remarks.

Palo Alto
Oct. 1972

# Contents

# Introduction

The marriage of sociology and mathematics, though many decades old, has always been difficult. In economics, the pioneering works of Walras, Pareto and others led with apparent ease to well-established research traditions. In sociology, interesting mathematical applications are easily detectable as early as the 18th century. However, it is not possible to speak of a continuous research tradition except during the last few decades.

An interesting hypothesis for the historian is perhaps the following: the mathematization of the social sciences may be considered as a three-stage process, the length of the three phases varying by discipline. In the first phase, isolated mathematical tools, generally rather rough and in most cases borrowed from other sciences, *e.g.* physics or biology, are used to solve isolated problems. Examples of this first phase include the tentative application of Newton's gravitational law to social migrations and of the logistic curve to social diffusion processes. Generally, attempts of this kind are likely to be accepted by the social science community with a certain amount of scepticism. These attempts are usually unable to change the traditional way of thinking about the phenomena with which they deal. They appear, so to speak, to be a foreign body in the traditional scientific thought.

After some time, however, these isolated attempts become more numerous and the mathematical tools, no longer borrowed, become more refined and sophisticated. Still more important, the mathematical social scientist gives up the "application" approach and takes a "formalization" approach, *i.e.* he tries to give a mathematical formulation to a given set of verbal or intuitive statements, rather than simply attempting to apply pre-existing mathematical tools or laws.

1

Finally, if this second phase is successful, a third phase is reached in which everyone is convinced that the mathematical language is indispensable.

If we are ready to accept the rough evolutionist theory presented above, we may say that many applications of mathematics to sociology still belong to phase 1. Perhaps phase 3 has been reached in some very exceptional cases. But there are also interesting cases located in phase 2, *i.e.* the phase in which the mathematical tools are already sufficiently original, numerous and autonomous to begin to convince people that empirical research, as well as theoretical thinking, are increasingly difficult without the help of mathematics. Social mobility belongs undoubtedly to this category.

This implies that, while it is not yet possible to speak of a well-integrated mathematical theory of mobility, we have already left the stage in which the mathematical tools used in this field can reasonably be considered as mere toys with only a speculative interest and without direct bearing on research, either empirical or theoretical. As we shall see, it is not very difficult to show that many bodies of mobility data cannot be properly analyzed without some mathematics. On the other hand, some theoretical problems, *e.g.* the problem of the effect on social mobility of the tremendous increase in the rates of school attendance which characterize the industrial societies, are satisfactorily dealt with in a verbal way. However, it becomes increasingly clear that the use of mathematics leads to a promising and more powerful kind of analysis at this theoretical level as well.

If our contention, that mathematical social mobility research belongs to the second phase of the evolutionary process, is true, this implies, first, that an overview of this research is certainly essential for any social mobility student. It also means that further study both of mathematical models and of the interrelationship between mathematics and empirical/theoretical research is needed before we reach the stage at which we can adequately speak of a mathematical theory of social mobility.

This general view leads to a number of expository principles. First, we have tried to make the presentation non-technical in order that the book be readable not only for mathematical sociologists but also for any social scientist with a minimal training in mathematics. The mathematical tools used are for the most part elementary, requiring only a good basis in matrix notation and matrix algebra and no differential calculus. Some of the models presented have continuous versions involving differential equations; but we have chosen to present only the discrete time versions.

Secondly, we have tried to provide the reader with an overview of mathematical tools or models used in social mobility research.

Finally, we have tried to be not only informative but also stimulating. This means that we have rejected a presentation of these mathematical tools as a mere list treating them on an equalitarian basis. We have tried to present them in an organized rather than in a taxonomic way. In other words, we have attempted to identify the main trends of research in this field, as well as the major steps forward that have appeared. This explains why some procedures are extensively presented and others are simply alluded to. While this procedure certainly involves some arbitrariness, it serves the purpose of presenting the main milestones of the intricate network considered. An exhaustive exposition of the already numerous mathematical models related to social mobility would certainly have contradicted our first principle, since each of these models would have had to be dealt with in a very condensed form.

In summary, this book has been conceived with the perspective of being useful on the one hand for students of social mobility, whatever their orientation, formal or substantive, and on the other hand for any social scientist interested in the development of mathematical thinking in sociology. Indeed, an expanding mathematical mobility theory has not only the effect of giving better insight into social mobility processes, but also of providing an illuminating example of the interest of mathematics for the social sciences generally. This theory is, however, far from being complete. On the contrary, much further formal research is needed. This openness is certainly stimulating for anyone interested in the development toward greater accuracy and power of the "language of social research".

Now, a word about what is understood by the label "social mobility". In handbooks on social mobility, several distinctions are usually introduced: horizontal *vs.* vertical mobility, intra- *vs.* intergenerational mobility, geographical *vs.* social mobility (although geographical mobility is also a form of social mobility), professional *vs.* social mobility, etc.

While these distinctions are essential from the substantive point of view, they become much more flexible when considered from a formal point of view. As we shall see, some models have been explicitly devised for a special class of situations, *e.g.* intragenerational mobility. But they may frequently be adapted to other

3

situations, *e.g.* intergenerational mobility. On the other hand, the level of generality of some models is such that they may be applied to any kind of mobility problem: many measurement models belong to this category.

The only class of models we shall explicitly exclude is that dealing exclusively with geographical mobility. Dodd's (1950), Stouffer's (1962) or Courgeau's (1970) works, among others, belong to this category. While they also deal with social mobility from a substantive point of view, we shall not consider them since, from a formal point of view, they use a very different mathematical approach. In the traditional social mobility approach, the basic formal atom, so to speak, is represented by what is usually called a mobility matrix, *i.e.* a table describing the moves of a set of individuals within a set of social categories during a given time period. All social mobility research (in the narrow sense of the phrase) makes use of this basic atom. In geographical mobility studies, this basic representation can also be and has actually been used: in this case, the social categories take the meaning of discrete spatial locations. But in many cases, distance is considered naturally as a continuous variable so that the matrix representation must be dropped. The mathematical models belonging to this category take the form of equations relating some dependent measure of geographical movements to the spatial distance covered by these movements.

The book has been divided into two parts. The first deals with measurement problems. These problems derive directly from the objectives of many mobility studies. Indeed, after the second World War, when empirical mobility research became proliferous, a major aim of the researchers was often either to study the international differences in the rates of mobility (*e.g.* is mobility greater in the U.S. than in Europe?) or to analyze mobility trends (is mobility increasing or decreasing with time?). These substantive problems led, as we shall see, to the difficult formal problem of building an acceptable index of mobility. This was necessary in order that the comparisons between mobility tables rest on a sound logical basis.

Later, partly as a consequence of this first type of research, some scientists noticed that a mobility process could be represented by the mathematical theory of stochastic processes. This gave rise to many models, the number of which has become increasingly important in the last few years. Most of these models lead to very interesting results for various problems, *e.g.* the effect of social mobility on social structures, or, more significantly, the

4

effect of social structures on social mobility, relationships between differential fertility and mobility, between the increase in the rates of school attendance and mobility, etc. All these models may be considered as particular steps toward a future, but presently incomplete, theory of social mobility.

These models constitute the material of our second part: "towards a formal theory of social mobility". Let us note, however, that the first and second parts of the book are not unconnected. On the one hand, the mathematical theory of stochastic processes has been used for theoretical purposes partly, as we saw, as a consequence of the efforts made to solve the measurement problem. On the other hand, in some cases, the definition of new mobility indices was precisely a by-product of attempts to build a formal theory of social mobility. Thus, some models could equally be presented either in the first or in the second part. Our somewhat arbitrary decision on this point derives from a subjective evaluation of whether the main interest of a given model lies more in its theoretical or in its measurement aspects.

The actual or potential substantive applications or illustrations of the models presented below are only suggested in most cases. The first reason for this is that a detailed presentation of applications would consume as much space as the description of the models themselves. The second reason is that it is impossible to describe exhaustively the field of application of a model. Thus, presenting a particular application could give a false idea of the potentialities of the model. This decision makes the book more abstract than it might have been. But the clear understanding of the logical foundations of a model seems to us to be essential before proceeding to apply it.

Being essentially a survey, the present book makes no attempt to discuss thoroughly the relationship between the sociological theory of mobility and mathematical mobility models. However, the reader will note that all models imply a particular mobility  theory. The idea of applying Markov chains to mobility analysis is, for instance, a natural one. But as soon as we do so, we introduce the implicit and probably undesirable postulate that change in the social structure is the product of the moves of individuals. For this reason, Markov chains have seldom been used in empirical research on mobility. The same is true of the numerous pseudo-Markovian models proposed in the literature for, although they eliminate a number of unrealistic assumptions of ordinary Markov chains,  they maintain the postulate according to which mobility determines the social structure. As a result, empirical research has turned to alternative kinds of tools such as multiple regression and other statistical methods. But, as I have tried to show elsewhere*, from a sociological point of view these statistical methods also introduce undesirable assumptions.

Certainly, the crucial problem is to bring mathematical research on mobility closer to sociological theory. What this means is very simple: we know, for instance, that such factors as education and fertility play an important role in mobility processes. We know also that people are not generally able to occupy jobs just because they are qualified to fill them. The jobs have also to exist. In other words, social structure is one of the explanatory factors of mobility and mobility should be considered as the result, at the *aggregative* level, of individuals' moves limited by social constraints (education, structure of opportunity) and by the moves of all other individuals. Many such "theoretical" requirements could be mentioned. Clearly, taking them into account is a necessary condition for mathematical models to have an impact on research and theory.

Another deliberate shortcoming of the book is that the statistical estimation problems raised by most of the models presented have been ignored. One of the reasons for this is that, in some cases, these problems are still unsolved. But the chief reason is again that our main purpose is to concentrate on the logic of the models, on their structure, on the relationship of their axioms with the real world, rather than to consider the technical problems of their applications to empirical data. The mathematical aspects of a model and the estimation problems raised can always be treated separately, undoubtedly representing two distinct steps. Whatever the practical importance of the second step, it may be provisionally ignored in a general book of this kind. However, some models, because they use a number of parameters smaller than the number of degrees of freedom included in the empirical information they account for, cannot be solved without the help of statistics. These statistical problems are dealt with in an appendix to the volume.

Finally, in order to make the text more easily readable, we have tried to use a systematic and homogeneous notation. Matrices are always described by capital bold-face letters, vectors by lower case bold-face letters. Some recurring concepts, such as transition matrices, turnover matrices, number of categories, etc. are described by fixed symbols. However, because of the great number of models which have been presented, it has been impossible to avoid some changes in the notation from one chapter to another.

* Boudon (1973b).

6

# Part 1: Measurement

# CHAPTER 1

## Social Mobility Measurement: Measures Without Models

### 1.1. Introductory remarks

As mentioned in the Introduction, the problem of social mobility measurement was first raised in connection with the needs of empirical research. As the works of Glass (1954), Lipset and Bendix (1960), Rogoff (1953), Carlsson (1958), and others have shown, a problem often raised by empirical research is to compare mobility matrices either for different countries or for different times. This problem has induced the derivation of mobility indices in order to obtain a basis for inter-matrix comparisons.

*Notation*

Let us first set up a system of notation which will be useful in the development which follows. Take, for instance, the case of an intergenerational mobility matrix, *i.e.* a matrix giving the cross-classification of father—son pairs by the social status of the father and that of the son, which may be represented as in Table 1.1. The number of father—son pairs with both members belonging to social status 1 will be $n_{11}$; the number of pairs with fathers in status 2 and sons in status 1 will be $n_{21}$; etc. On the other hand, $n_{1.}$ is the number of pairs with fathers in status 1 (which may differ from the number of fathers in status 1, since a particular father may be paired with several sons, and thus counted several

7

TABLE 1.1

Notations for a turnover mobility matrix

| Social status of the fathers | Social status of the sons | | | | | Total |
|---|---|---|---|---|---|---|
| | 1 | 2 | ... $i$ | ... | $\sigma$ | |
| 1 | $n_{11}$ | $n_{12}$ ... | $n_{1i}$ ... | | $n_{1\sigma}$ | $n_{1.}$ |
| 2 | $n_{21}$ | $n_{22}$ ... | $n_{2i}$ ... | | $n_{2\sigma}$ | $n_{2.}$ |
| | ............................................. | | | | | |
| $j$ | $n_{j1}$ | $n_{j2}$ ... | $n_{ji}$ ... | | $n_{j\sigma}$ | $n_{j.}$ |
| | ............................................. | | | | | |
| $\sigma$ | $n_{\sigma 1}$ | $n_{\sigma 2}$ ... | $n_{\sigma i}$ ... | | $n_{\sigma\sigma}$ | $n_{\sigma.}$ |
| Total | $n_{.1}$ | $n_{.2}$ ... | $n_{.i}$ ... | | $n_{.\sigma}$ | $N$ |

times); and $n_{.1}$ is the number of pairs with sons in status 1; etc. The total number of father—son pairs is denoted $N$.

In many applications, division of all the quantities of this matrix by $N$, is useful. With

$$p_{ij} = \frac{n_{ij}}{N} \tag{1.1}$$

we have Table 1.2, which may be called a proportion turnover matrix. The interpretation of this matrix is the same as above, except that all the quantities appearing in Table 1.2 are proportions.

Then, the turnover matrices can be characterized by

$$\sum_{i,j} n_{ij} = N \tag{1.2}$$

when dealing with the counts and by

$$\sum_{i,j} p_{ij} = 1 \tag{1.3}$$

when dealing with proportions.

In many cases, consideration of transition matrices rather than

TABLE 1.2

Proportion turnover matrix

| Social status of fathers | Social status of sons | | | | | Total |
|---|---|---|---|---|---|---|
| | 1 | 2 ... | $i$ | ... | $\sigma$ | |
| 1 | $p_{11}$ | $p_{12}$ ... | $p_{1i}$ ... | | $p_{1\sigma}$ | $p_{1.}$ |
| 2 | $p_{21}$ | $p_{22}$ ... | $p_{2i}$ ... | | $p_{2\sigma}$ | $p_{2.}$ |
| ............................................ | | | | | | |
| $j$ | $p_{j1}$ | $p_{j2}$ ... | $p_{ji}$ ... | | $p_{j\sigma}$ | $p_{j.}$ |
| ............................................ | | | | | | |
| $\sigma$ | $p_{\sigma 1}$ | $p_{\sigma 2}$ ... | $p_{\sigma i}$ ... | | $p_{\sigma\sigma}$ | $p_{\sigma.}$ |
| Total | $P_{.1}$ | $P_{.2}$ ... | $P_{.i}$ ... | | $P_{.\sigma}$ | 1 |

turnover matrices is useful. A transition matrix is derived from a turnover matrix by dividing all the elements of the latter by the corresponding row totals. Thus, the $(i,j)$ element of a transition matrix is

$$r_{ij} = \frac{n_{ij}}{n_{i.}} = \frac{p_{ij}}{p_{i.}} \tag{1.4}$$

so that

$$\sum_j r_{ij} = 1 \tag{1.5}$$

In other words, a transition matrix has all its row totals equal to 1 and $r_{ij}$ describes the conditional probability of going to $j$ from $i$. The notation for a general transition matrix is given in Table 1.3.

*Interpretation of intergenerational mobility tables*

Since we shall deal extensively with intergenerational mobility tables, a few comments may be introduced at this point on the logical problems they raise. As mentioned above, an important proportion of the data collected in the field of social mobility takes the form of these intergenerational mobility matrices.

Many criticisms have, however, been raised against the widely

9

TABLE 1.3

Transition matrix

| Social status of fathers | Social status of sons | | | | | | Total |
|---|---|---|---|---|---|---|---|
| | 1 | 2 | ... | $i$ | ... | $\sigma$ | |
| 1 | $r_{11}$ | $r_{12}$ | $\cdots$ | $r_{1i}$ | $\cdots$ | $r_{1\sigma}$ | 1 |
| 2 | $r_{21}$ | $r_{22}$ | $\cdots$ | $r_{2i}$ | $\cdots$ | $r_{2\sigma}$ | 1 |
| $j$ | $r_{j1}$ | $r_{j2}$ | $\cdots$ | $r_{ji}$ | $\cdots$ | $r_{j\sigma}$ | 1 |
| $\sigma$ | $r_{\sigma1}$ | $r_{\sigma2}$ | $\cdots$ | $r_{\sigma i}$ | $\cdots$ | $r_{\sigma\sigma}$ | 1 |

used data-gathering techniques leading to this kind of table. The most complete critical view is contained in a paper by Duncan (1966). We shall summarize it briefly.

(1) Generally, an intergenerational mobility matrix (IMM) is constructed by taking a sample of sons and asking them about their father's occupation.

(2) However much caution is used in building the observation design, unavoidable interpretation problems arise.

(3) One of these problems results, for instance, from the fact that two sons in the sample generally have fathers with different ages. The fathers are likely to have started their last or main occupation at different times. This is important in an approach where social mobility is considered at least partly as a consequence of the social structures. The composition of the labor force, and consequently the occupational opportunities, may have been different at these two points in time. On the other hand, if the respondents are asked about their father's occupation at a given time, the information will correspond to different points in occupational careers.

(4) Differential fertility will lead to an over-representation of fathers of the more fertile social categories in the pseudo-sample.

In other words, whatever the logical adequacy of the measures applied to such an IMM, they will have to be interpreted carefully. A nominalist solution to these difficulties would be to follow Duncan's suggestion and consider the IMM not as information on mobility; but merely as information on the dependence of sons' statuses on fathers' statuses. A pragmatic solution would be to consider the IMM as containing valid information on mobility and to interpret cautiously the measures associated with these tables (for instance by taking into account, exclusively, sufficiently large differences, etc.).

Another solution would be to use other types of observational methods, *e.g.* cohort or panel designs. But this raises obvious practical problems in the case of intergenerational mobility.

*Types of indices*

Several categories of indices may be distinguished. Some are directly derived from the concept of mobility without the help of a mathematical model. We shall call these direct measures. In this class one may distinguish, on the one hand, pragmatic measures which are proposed on the basis of a rough relationship between the mobility concept and some of the parameters which may be used to describe a mobility table, and, on the other hand, measures which derive from a formalization of the mobility concept.

A survey of these direct measures, both pragmatic and formal is given in the following sections of Chapter 1. It seems necessary to have a rather lengthy presentation of these measures because of their relevance in empirical research. The results drawn from the numerous empirical studies on comparative social mobility both in time and in space are closely related to the quality of the parametrization used to compare mobility tables. Problems produced by this parametrization provide a useful introduction to the more elaborate mathematical tools presented in the following chapters. Also, these measurement problems were historically raised first. The applications of mathematical models to social mobility were derived originally from the difficulties encountered in trying to solve these problems.

In Chapter 2, we shall deal with measures derived from mathematical models. This will provide an opportunity not only of presenting more elaborate measures, but also of introducing some elementary mathematical processes. Thus, Chapter 2 may be considered both as concluding the first part of this book on measurement and as introducing the theoretical second part.

## 1.2. Pragmatic measures

In order to approach the mobility measurement problem, consideration of the simple dichotomous table, *i.e.* an IMM with $\sigma=2$, where social status 1, for instance, represents the category of manual workers, and status 2 the category of non-manual workers (Tables 1.4 and 1.5), may be useful.

TABLE 1.4

Dichotomous turnover. IMM using counts

| Father's status | Son's status | | |
|---|---|---|---|
| | 1 | 2 | |
| 1 | $n_{11}$ | $n_{12}$ | $n_{1.}$ |
| 2 | $n_{21}$ | $n_{22}$ | $n_{2.}$ |
| | $n_{.1}$ | $n_{.2}$ | $N$ |

TABLE 1.5

Dichotomous turnover. IMM using proportions

| Father's status | Son's status | | |
|---|---|---|---|
| | 1 | 2 | |
| 1 | $p_{11}$ | $p_{12}$ | $p_{1.}$ |
| 2 | $p_{21}$ | $p_{22}$ | $p_{2.}$ |
| | $p_{.1}$ | $p_{.2}$ | 1 |

*Crude measures*

Many very simple indices of mobility may be, and have actually been, associated with tables such as these. Let us consider for instance $n_{11}/n_{1.}$, the proportion of manual fathers with manual sons. While, strictly speaking, this quantity is nothing more than what it says, it may in some cases be interpreted as an overall immobility index. The greater or lesser ease of climbing from a manual to a non-manual occupation is an essential feature which may be considered to characterize the mobility of a society as a whole. However, such an interpretation raises many problems. Thus, $n_{22}/n_{2.}$, the proportion of non-manual fathers with non-manual sons, may also be interpreted as an overall measure of immobility. Now generally

$$\frac{n_{11}}{n_{1.}} \neq \frac{n_{22}}{n_{2.}} \tag{1.6}$$

The question is still more complicated since $n_{11}/n_{.1}$ and $n_{22}/n_{.2}$, respectively the proportion of lower class sons with lower class fathers and of higher class sons with higher class fathers, can also be considered as overall immobility indices. Of course, all four of these quantities are related to one another since a dichotomous table has only one degree of freedom once the marginals are fixed. But this general statement does not answer the following questions.

(1) Which one of these quantities should be preferred to the others?

(2) Under what circumstances, if any, one should be preferred to the others? We shall see below (Section 1.4) that these questions may possibly be given a definitive answer. Of course, in order to do so, a more accurate mathematical analysis is needed.

Another pragmatic measure is $(n_{12} + n_{21})/N$, the proportion of mobiles. This is an index of mobility while the complementary proportion of immobiles, $(n_{11} + n_{22})/N$, is the corresponding immobility index. The same remarks as before apply here. While the latter quantity is, strictly speaking, nothing more than the proportion of immobiles, it may be interpreted as an overall immobility index. But this interpretation also raises many problems. Thus, a society with a high overall increase in non-manual occupations during a generation will generate automatically a certain proportion of mobiles. Thus, from the point of view of mobility, this society will be different from another in which the overall increase in non-manual occupations is smaller, even if both show the same proportion of mobiles. Formally, it is dangerous to use the proportion of mobiles as a mobility index, except if the marginal trends are the same for all the mobility tables to be compared (but what do we mean precisely by "the same" here?). Otherwise, we must eliminate the effects of the differences in trends (but how?).

13

Let us now consider a large family of indices, all characterized by the core concept of perfect mobility.

*Elementary measures using perfect mobility*

One of the most popular and also most discussed indices in this family was proposed by the British sociologist Glass (1954). The rationale for this index is the following: if, in a society, the amount of mobility is maximum, the social status of a son should be independent of the social status of his father. In other words, the proportion of sons with status 1 should be the same, whatever the status of the father. In the dichotomous case which we are considering, this condition of perfect mobility is described by

$$\frac{p_{11}}{p_{1.}} = \frac{p_{21}}{p_{2.}} \tag{1.7}$$

or

$$\frac{p_{11}}{p_{1.}} - \frac{p_{21}}{p_{2.}} = 0 \tag{1.8}$$

Reducing to the same denominator and rearranging terms leads to the definition of perfect mobility

$$p_{11} = p_{1.} p_{.1} \tag{1.9}$$

or

$$N n_{11} = n_{1.} n_{.1} \tag{1.10}$$

If eqn. (1.9) holds, the son's status does not depend on his father's status. If $p_{11}$ is greater than $p_{1.} p_{.1}$, the proportion of sons with status 1 is greater when the father also has status 1. If $p_{11}$ happens to be smaller than $p_{1.} p_{.1}$, the proportion of sons with status 1 is smaller when the father has status 1. The latter situation was considered by Glass as irrelevant, since it is unlikely to occur in normal situations.

This leads naturally to the definition of the immobility index used by Glass

$$I_G = \frac{p_{11}}{p_{1.} p_{.1}} = \frac{N n_{11}}{n_{1.} n_{.1}} \tag{1.11}$$

Of course, a parallel index could be constructed for social status 2. Generally, with $\sigma$ statuses, the immobility characterizing the $i$-th status will be defined by

$$I_{G(i)} = \frac{p_{ii}}{p_{i.}p_{.i}} = \frac{Nn_{ii}}{n_{i.}n_{.i}} \qquad (1.12)$$

Finally, it is easy to define complementary mobility (rather than immobility) indices. The complementary index to eqn. (1.11) would be

$$M_G = \frac{p_{12}}{p_{1.}p_{.2}} = \frac{Nn_{12}}{n_{1.}n_{.2}} \qquad (1.13)$$

while the complementary index to eqn. (1.12) would be

$$M_{G(i)} = \frac{p_{i.} - p_{ii}}{p_{i.}(1 - p_{.i})}$$

$$= \frac{N(n_{i.} - n_{ii})}{n_{i.}(N - n_{.i})} \qquad (1.14)$$

However, a number of authors have shown that the Glass index raises many problems. Without going into detailed examination of these criticisms, we shall use a simple arithmetic example which shows that this index may, in some cases, be misleading.

TABLE 1.6

Fictitious IMM with maximum immobility *from status 1*

| Father's status | Son's status | | |
|---|---|---|---|
| | 1 | 2 | |
| 1 | 80 | 0 | 80 |
| 2 | 100 | 20 | 120 |
| | 180 | 20 | 200 |

TABLE 1.7

Fictitious IMM with non-maximum immobility

| Father's status | Son's status | | |
|---|---|---|---|
| | 1 | 2 | |
| 1 | 80 | 20 | 100 |
| 2 | 20 | 80 | 100 |
| | 100 | 100 | 200 |

Let us consider the fictitious Tables 1.6 and 1.7. If we look at Table 1.6, we have the impression of strong or even maximum immobility: all sons with father from social status 1 also have this status. Table 1.7, on the other hand, suggests a much more liberal picture: 20 among the 100 sons with fathers from status 1 belong to status 2. At the least, Table 1.7 is not characterized by maximum immobility. In other words, Table 1.7 describes a more mobile society than Table 1.6.

If we compute the Glass immobility index for these tables, however, we find for Table 1.6: $I_G$ = (200)(80)/(80)(180) = 1.11, and for Table 1.7: $I_G$ = (200)(80)/(100)(100) = 1.60. Thus, the index tells us that immobility should be considered greater in Table 1.7. This clearly contradicts what we expect on an intuitive basis.

It is rather easy to see where the difficulty lies. Table 1.6 is characterized by an important structural move: the composition of the labor force is very different from one generation to the next. Table 1.7, on the other hand, shows a complete structural stability. Thus, the Glass index is actually a heterogenous measure. It measures, at the same time, that part of total mobility independent of structural changes in the composition of the labor force and that part of total mobility due to these changes.

*Rogoff's interpretation of the Glass index*

It is interesting to discuss briefly the interpretation given by Rogoff (1953), of the Glass index. In her empirical work, Rogoff has shown that, in the period she examined, the increase in the number of skilled workers' sons becoming lower white-collar workers was due, not to a greater facility of moving up from the lower status to the higher, but to a greater demand for white-collar workers. Thus, she concluded that, in order to measure true mobility, this demand factor must be accounted for.

Let us consider again the dichotomous case. The demand for status 2 workers may be measured by $n_{.2}/N$. On the other hand, $n_{12}/n_{1.}$, the proportion of sons with social origin 1 having current status 2, may be considered as a crude indicator of mobility. In order to refine this indicator, Rogoff proposes to introduce the demand $n_{.2}/N$ as a correction factor: the greater the demand, the smaller the amount of mobility not generated by the latter. Hence the index of mobility proposed by Rogoff is

16

$$M_G = \frac{n_{12}/n_{1.}}{n_{.2}/N}$$

$$= \frac{Nn_{12}}{n_{1.}n_{.2}} \qquad (1.15)$$

This is exactly the Glass mobility index defined in eqn. (1.13). Thus, eqn. (1.15) is essentially a useful alternative interpretation of the Glass index.

The stimulating side to the derivation of eqn. (1.15) is the clear stress on the idea that a good mobility index should make a distinction between the amount of mobility generated by the changes in the social structure and the amount of mobility generated by other factors. Indeed, the former should be eliminated. Rogoff's index does not actually make the distinction since it is identical to the Glass index. But its presentation has a clear heuristic bearing.

Let us note, incidentally, that the usual correlation or regression coefficients for dichotomous variables do not settle the problem of mobility measurement either. The regression coefficient, $f$, and the correlation coefficient, $\varphi$, computed for Table 1.6 are far from their maximum value of +1, although immobility is maximum in this table. Yule's $Q$ is at least apparently more adequate. However, it is not difficult to devise fictitious tables where $Q$ would lead to unsatisfactory results. Of course, $Q$ is an ad hoc coefficient without a well-defined mathematical basis.

Finally, another weakness of the Glass—Rogoff index should be noted: its maximum value is dependent on the marginals.

## 1.3. Distinguishing between structural and pure mobility

A first possible answer to the problem raised but not solved by Rogoff's index was proposed by Yasuda (1964).

*Yasuda's index*

The rationale for this index is the following.

(1) Let us call *structural mobility* the amount of mobility generated by the fact that the distribution among social strata experienced by the sons differs from the corresponding experience of their fathers at the various times in the past for which the fathers' statuses were recorded.

17

(2) Let us define *pure* or *exchange mobility* as the part of the total mobility which is not structural.

The index rests, in other words, upon the basic decomposition

Pure mobility = total mobility — structural mobility

A brief comment may be introduced here. It must be noted that the previous distinction between structural and pure mobility should not be interpreted too literally. Indeed, if the number of social positions of a given category, say $n_{1.}$, does not change from one point in time to the next, this certainly does not exclude some social positions of category 1 being created while others are eliminated. Thus, the apparent lack of structural change will, in fact, generally conceal the existence of many structural changes forcing people out of some jobs and into others. The structural mobility to be defined below using the marginals of a mobility table is thus an abstract notion: it may be interpreted as an indicator of the actual amount of structural mobility.

Let us first consider the case of a dichotomous table which has the advantage of being the simplest one (as we shall see, indices for polytomies are natural extensions of those for dichotomies: exposition is thus facilitated by considering dichotomies first). The definitions are as follows.

Total mobility = $n_{1.} - n_{11}$

Structural or forced out mobility = $n_{1.} - \min(n_{1.}, n_{.1})$

and hence

Pure mobility = $n_{1.} - n_{11} - n_{1.} + \min(n_{1.}, n_{.1})$

$$= \min(n_{1.}, n_{.1}) - n_{11}$$

Needless to say, a symmetric index might also be constructed starting from the opposite corner of the mobility table. The relation between these symmetric indices would be the same as the relation between two symmetric correlation coefficients, *i.e.* they would be identical. We shall return to this point later.

The pure mobility, as defined above, cannot, of course, be used as a measure of mobility directly, since this quantity is clearly not independent of the marginals. Then, the next step taken by Yasuda is to refer this observed pure mobility to the theoretical

18

pure mobility which would be generated by the same marginals in a situation of perfect mobility. This latter quantity is equal to

$$\min(n_{1.}, n_{.1}) - \frac{n_{1.} n_{.1}}{N}$$

Finally, Yasuda's mobility index, which we shall call $M_Y$, is defined by

$$M_Y = \frac{\min(n_{1.}, n_{.1}) - n_{11}}{\min(n_{1.}, n_{.1}) - (n_{1.} n_{.1}/N)} \tag{1.16}$$

The complementary immobility index is

$$I_Y = 1 - M_Y = 1 - \frac{\min(n_{1.}, n_{.1}) - n_{11}}{\min(n_{1.}, n_{.1}) - (n_{1.} n_{.1}/N)}$$

$$= \frac{n_{11} - (n_{1.} n_{.1}/N)}{\min(n_{1.}, n_{.1}) - (n_{1.} n_{.1}/N)} \tag{1.17}$$

Applying this index to Tables 1.6 and 1.7, we find that the immobility which characterizes Table 1.6 is 1, while that for Table 1.7 is 0.60. These figures are more satisfactory than the results derived from the Glass index.

*Relation between the Glass and Yasuda indices*

Note that, although Yasuda's index is mathematically very close to the Glass index, it leads to definitely different results.

Let us return to eqn. (1.16) and look at the two possible assumptions about $\min(n_{1.}, n_{.1})$.

(1) $\min(n_{1.}, n_{.1}) = n_{1.}$

In this case

$$M_Y = \frac{n_{1.} - n_{11}}{n_{1.} - (n_{1.} n_{.1}/N)}$$

$$= \frac{n_{12}}{n_{1.} n_{.2}/N} = \frac{N n_{12}}{n_{1.} n_{.2}} \tag{1.18a}$$

(2) $\min(n_{1.}, n_{.1}) = n_{.1}$

19

In this case

$$M_Y = \frac{n_{.1} - n_{11}}{n_{.1} - (n_{1.}n_{.1}/N)}$$

$$= \frac{n_{21}}{n_{.1}n_{2.}/N} = \frac{Nn_{21}}{n_{.1}n_{2.}} \qquad (1.18b)$$

This leads to the synthetic definition

$$M_Y = \frac{Nn_{ij}}{n_{i.}n_{.j}}$$

with

$$i = 1, \ j = 2, \ \text{if } n_{1.} \leqslant n_{.1}$$
$$i = 2, \ j = 1, \ \text{if } n_{.1} \leqslant n_{1.} \qquad (1.19)$$

Comparison of eqns. (1.19) and (1.13) shows that Yasuda's mobility index will be the same as the Glass index when $\min(n_{1.}, n_{.1}) = n_{1.}$. It will generally be different otherwise. If $\min(n_{1.}, n_{.1}) = n_{.1}$, the Glass index retains its validity if subscripts 1 and 2 are permuted in eqn. (1.13).

As mentioned above, an index symmetric to $M_Y$ may be defined by starting from the opposite corner of the dichotomous mobility table. We have, in this case, the following definitions.

Total mobility $= n_{2.} - n_{22}$

Structural mobility $= n_{2.} - \min(n_{2.}, n_{.2})$

This symmetric index, say $M_Y'$, will be the same as $M_Y$ except that subscripts 1 and 2 will be permuted. Thus, from eqn. (1.19) we obtain

$$M_Y' = \frac{Nn_{ij}}{n_{i.}n_{.j}}$$

with

$$i = 2, \ j = 1, \ \text{if } n_{2.} \leqslant n_{.2}$$
$$i = 1, \ j = 2, \ \text{if } n_{.2} \leqslant n_{2.} \qquad (1.20)$$

But, since

$$n_{2.} \leqslant n_{.2} \Rightarrow n_{.1} \leqslant n_{1.}$$

$$n_{.2} \leqslant n_{2.} \Rightarrow n_{1.} \leqslant n_{.1}$$

eqns. (1.19) and (1.20) are not distinct. Thus

$$M_Y = M_Y{}' \qquad\qquad (1.21)$$

*Application to non-dichotomous mobility tables*

In the non-dichotomous mobility case, Yasuda proposes the following immobility index

$$I_Y{}^G = \frac{\displaystyle\sum_i n_{ii} - \sum_i (n_{i.} n_{.i}/N)}{\displaystyle\sum_i \min(n_{i.}, n_{.i}) - \sum_i (n_{i.} n_{.i}/N)} \qquad (1.22)$$

*[handwritten margin notes: "isn't this wrong? No. See Yasuda's eq. 3."]*

the summation being extended over all strata. By eqn. (1.21), it may easily be verified that $I_Y{}^G$ is equal to $I_Y$ when $\sigma = 2$. However, as can be seen by comparing eqns. (1.17) and (1.22), this is a straightforward but also ad hoc generalization. While the conceptual meaning of eqn. (1.17) is perfectly clear, the same does not hold for eqn. (1.22), which has been produced simply by an averaging procedure applied to the dichotomous formulation.

Yasuda has applied his index to various sets of empirical data. He has shown, for instance, that the image, drawn by his index of the mobility of various social strata in Japan is very different from that resulting from the application of the Glass index. Also, the surprising results of Lipset and Bendix, according to which mobility is almost the same in various western societies, are seriously challenged when Yasuda's index is used.

Little doubt exists that Yasuda's index is much more satisfactory than the indices previously discussed. This results from the fact that the dissociation between structural and pure mobility is not only stressed, but also rigorously formulated. The comparative statements drawn from this index are more likely to be valid than the statements drawn from less adequate indices.

A slight logical problem is raised by the limits of $M_Y$. In the case of complete immobility, $M_Y$ will be zero. It will be 1 in the case of perfect mobility. But, logically if not practically, the amount of mobility may be more than perfect. Therefore, if we ignore for a moment its substantive meaning, $M_Y$ has no well-defined upper limit. This contradicts the generally accepted

21

methodological rules used in index building. Consequently, even if $M_Y$, in practice, is very unlikely to be greater than 1, its values can be validly interpreted at the ordinal level, but not at the interval level. This may have some relevance, especially when dealing with longitudinal comparisons. Suppose for instance that, taking three mobility matrices at five year intervals, we find the values 0.55, 0.61 and 0.57, respectively for $M_Y$. The only result we can draw from these figures is that mobility increased and then decreased. No meaning can be given to the differences between these figures. In other words, it is difficult to say whether they suggest an oscillatory or a decreasing trend.

## 1.4. Dropping perfect mobility

The author (1972) has proposed an alternative index of social mobility which retains the idea of a separation between structural and pure mobility, but drops the reference point of perfect mobility. Let us call this index $M_B$ in its mobility version and $I_B$ in its immobility version.

### The rationale for $I_B$

In order to illustrate the rationale for this index, let us consider the fictitious dichotomous Tables 1.8 and 1.9 (polytomies will be considered later).

Table 1.8 appears to indicate strong social immobility: a large number of people remain in their original status category. This intuitive feeling may be conceptualized in the following way.

TABLE 1.8
Fictitious mobility table

| Father's status | Son's status | | |
|---|---|---|---|
| | 1 | 2 | |
| 1 | 280 | 120 | 400 |
| 2 | 20 | 80 | 100 |
| | 300 | 200 | 500 |

TABLE 1.9

Another fictitious mobility table

| Father's status | Son's status | | |
|---|---|---|---|
| | 1 | 2 | |
| 1 | 280 | 20 | 300 |
| 2 | 120 | 80 | 200 |
| | 400 | 100 | 500 |

Suppose

(1) that a powerful decision maker (DM) is in charge of distributing the available social positions;

(2) that DM is in favor of creating a limited amount of mobility so that he will give people from status 1 many social positions of category 1 or, alternatively, give people from status 2 many social positions of category 2;

(3) that he is also prudent and does not want to appear too much prejudiced; and

(4) that he is not master of the marginals.

Let us suppose that DM starts filling the matrices considering first social category number 2. In Table 1.8, 100 class 2 people are competing for 200 positions in the same category. In Table 1.9, 200 class 2 people are competing for 100 positions of the same level. We shall suppose that for Table 1.8, DM locates $100x\%$ of the candidates from social category 2 in the same achievement category, while for Table 1.9, he gives $100x\%$ of the available social positions of category 2 to candidates from this category. In other words

$$x = \frac{n_{22}}{\min(n_{2.}, n_{.2})} \qquad (1.23)$$

summarizes the degree to which DM wants to minimize moves from one generation to the next. Of course, a symmetric parametrization is provided by

$$x' = \frac{n_{11}}{\min(n_{1.}, n_{.1})} \qquad (1.24)$$

We shall consider this problem later.

Parameter $x$ cannot be used directly as a measure of immobility. Indeed, while its maximum value is 1, its minimum value depends

23

x is the proportion of sons in category 2 with same status as fathers ?
— NOT QUITE !

on the marginals. Let us consider, for instance, Table 1.10 and suppose DM chooses $x = 0.20$. Given the marginals of this table, this generates a negative figure in the north-west cell of the table. Thus, $x$ has to be referred to its minimum value, say $x_{min}$.

TABLE 1.10

Case where some values of $x$ generate negative figures

| Father's status | Son's status | | |
|---|---|---|---|
| | 1 | 2 | |
| 1 | −40 | 240 | 200 |
| 2 | 240 | 60 | 300 |
| | 200 | 300 | 500 |

Now, the condition for no negative figures appearing in the cell (1,1) is

$$n_{11} \geqslant 0 \qquad (1.25)$$

or

$$n_{1.} - n_{12} = n_{1.} - (n_{.2} - n_{22})$$

$$= n_{1.} - n_{.2} + x \min(n_{2.}, n_{.2}) \geqslant 0 \qquad (1.26)$$

This implies

$$x \geqslant \frac{n_{.2} - n_{1.}}{\min(n_{2.}, n_{.2})} \qquad (1.27)$$

so that

$$x_{min} = \frac{(n_{.2} - n_{1.})^*}{\min(n_{2.}, n_{.2})}$$

with $(n_{.2} - n_{1.})^* = (n_{.2} - n_{1.})$ if this quantity is positive or 0 if it is not.

We can now define a standardized immobility index $I_B$ in the following way

$$I_B = \frac{x - x_{min}}{1 - x_{min}} \qquad (1.28)$$

By contrast with Yasuda's index, $I_B$ has well-defined limits. Its minimum value is 0 and its maximum value is 1.

Explicitly, the formula for $I_B$ is

$$I_B = \frac{[n_{22}/\min(n_{2.},n_{.2})] - [(n_{.2}-n_{1.})^*/\min(n_{2.},n_{.2})]}{1 - [(n_{.2}-n_{1.})^*/\min(n_{2.},n_{.2})]}$$

$$= \frac{n_{22} - (n_{.2}-n_{1.})^*}{\min(n_{2.},n_{.2}) - (n_{.2}-n_{1.})^*} \tag{1.29}$$

If $n_{.2} \leqslant n_{1.}$, the index takes the simple form

$$I_B = \frac{n_{22}}{\min(n_{2.},n_{.2})} \tag{1.30}$$

If $n_{.2} \geqslant n_{1.}$, we have

$$I_B = \frac{n_{22} - (n_{.2}-n_{1.})}{\min(n_{2.},n_{.2}) - (n_{.2}-n_{1.})}$$

$$= \frac{n_{1.} - n_{12}}{\min(n_{2.},n_{.2}) - (n_{.2}-n_{1.})} \tag{1.31}$$

Let us now suppose

$$n_{2.} \leqslant n_{.2} \tag{1.32}$$

In this case

$$I_B = \frac{n_{1.} - n_{12}}{N - n_{.2}} = \frac{n_{11}}{n_{.1}} \tag{1.33}$$

If, on the contrary, $n_{2.} \geqslant n_{.2}$

$$M_B = \frac{n_{1.} - n_{12}}{n_{1.}} = \frac{n_{11}}{n_{1.}} \tag{1.34}$$

But,

$$n_{2.} \leqslant n_{.2} \Rightarrow n_{.1} \leqslant n_{1.}$$
$$n_{2.} \geqslant n_{.2} \Rightarrow n_{.1} \geqslant n_{1.} \tag{1.35}$$

Thus, from eqns. (1.32)−(1.35), when $n_{.2} \geqslant n_{1.}$

$$I_B = \frac{n_{11}}{\min(n_{1.}, n_{.1})} \tag{1.36}$$

Finally, from eqns. (1.30) and (1.36), we obtain a synthetic formula for $I_B$.

$$I_B = \frac{n_{ii}}{\min(n_{i.}, n_{.i})}$$

with

$i = 1$  if $n_{1.} \leqslant n_{.2}$

$i = 2$  if $n_{1.} \geqslant n_{.2}$ $\tag{1.37}$

Thus, $I_B$ appears as a very simple, easily computed index. It is also very close to the crude intuitive index (1.6) described in Section 1.2, just as Yasuda's index is close to the Glass index. But the difference between the index (1.6) or Glass index on the one hand and the $I_B$ or Yasuda's index on the other is that the latter two take account of the relevant information contained in the marginals, while the former do not. It is interesting to look closely at the structure of eqn. (1.19) for the Yasuda index and of eqn. (1.37) for the index $I_B$. In both cases, the index is independent of the marginals in the sense that the formula for the index changes according to the structure of the marginals. This situation is very different, for instance, from the situation we meet in the case of correlation coefficients. In this latter case, independence with regard to the marginals is, so to speak, embodied in the correlation formula itself.

The formulas (1.19) and (1.37) also have an interesting methodological implication. They show that the indices which are currently used in the empirical literature on mobility, like index (1.6) or the Glass index, may sometimes be absolutely correct. This depends on whether the conditions which appear on the right hand side of eqns. (1.19) and (1.37) are satisfied or not. But they may also be incorrect.

Let us finally add two further points. First, it is obvious that

$$M_B = 1 - I_B \tag{1.38}$$

defines the mobility index corresponding to the immobility index $I_B$.

26

Secondly, an immobility index, say $I_B{}'$, might have been constructed starting from eqn. (1.24) rather than from eqn. (1.23). The only change in the derivation, (1.25) to (1.37), would have been to substitute the subscript 1 for 2 and 2 for 1. Now, permuting the subscripts 1 and 2 in eqn. (1.37) does not change the formula. In other words

$$I_B = I_B{}' \qquad\qquad (1.39)$$

so that the index $I_B$ like Yasuda's index, is symmetric in the sense that it may equally be derived starting from the lower-right cell of the mobility matrix and using eqn. (1.23) or from the upper-left cell and using eqn. (1.24).

*Comparison of Yasuda's index and $I_B$*

The structure of $I_B$ may be compared with that of $I_Y$, Yasuda's corresponding index.

Let us suppose for a moment that the decision maker (DM) introduced at the beginning of this section behaves exactly as before, choosing a value $x$ describing the proportion of sons from class 2 to obtain the social positions of class 2 or, alternatively the proportion of social positions 2 to be granted to these sons.

Let us also suppose that the action of DM is evaluated by two different minded observers $O_1$ and $O_2$. $O_1$ has no preconception whatever as to the right amount of mobility which should occur in a society. Thus, he will try to locate $x$ between its mathematical minimum and maximum values. He will, in other words, use eqn. (1.28). Observer $O_2$ on the other hand, is convinced that perfect mobility should be the point of reference for evaluating the decisions of DM. He will then use, not eqn. (1.28) but, say, $Z$ with

$$Z = \frac{x - x_{rand}}{1 - x_{rand}} \qquad\qquad (1.40)$$

Equation (1.40) is the same as eqn. (1.28) except that $x_{rand}$ replaces $x_{min}$. Then, $x_{rand}$ is the value of $x$ which would generate a perfect mobility table if it happened to be chosen by DM. If $x = x_{rand}$, $Z$ is 0 and the immobility is lowest with regard to the perfect mobility criterion.

It is readily verified that

$$x_{\text{rand}} = \frac{(n_{2.}n_{.2}/N)}{\min(n_{2.}, n_{.2})} \tag{1.41}$$

Substituting eqns. (1.23) and (1.41) into eqn. (1.40) yields

$$Z = \frac{n_{22}/\min(n_{2.}, n_{.2}) - (n_{2.}n_{.2}/N)/\min(n_{2.}, n_{.2})}{1 - (n_{2.}n_{.2}/N)/\min(n_{2.}, n_{.2})}$$

$$= \frac{n_{22} - (n_{2.}n_{.2}/N)}{\min(n_{2.}, n_{.2}) - (n_{2.}n_{.2}/N)} \tag{1.42}$$

Alternatively, it is possible to start from the upper left corner of the mobility matrix. This yields

$$Z = \frac{n_{11} - (n_{1.}n_{.1}/N)}{\min(n_{1.}, n_{.1}) - (n_{1.}n_{.1}/N)} \tag{1.43}$$

Now, if we compare eqn. (1.43) with eqn. (1.17), we see that $Z$ is no more than $I_Y$, Yasuda's immobility index.

Thus, $I_Y$ has the same structure as $I_B$, but a different reference point. In the case of $I_B$, the parameter $x$ is, so to speak, evaluated by taking, as a reference, the maximum possible amount of movement. In the case of Yasuda's index, $I_Y$, it is evaluated taking perfect mobility as the reference.

This raises the question of which of $I_Y$ or $I_B$ should be preferred. Our contention is that the latter is more content-free than the former, since $x_{\text{rand}}$ may only be considered as the minimum value of $x$ for substantive reasons and not for mathematical reasons. Of course, $x < x_{\text{rand}}$ should occur only exceptionally in practice (except in revolutionary periods). But it is hard to see very clearly why this consideration should be taken into account. Nobody would think, for instance, of measuring the proportion of giants in a set of societies by defining a specific measure, even if this proportion is very unlikely to reach, say, even 0.02.

Besides the ease of computation, $I_B$ (or its complement, $M_B$) also has the advantage, as compared with Yasuda's index, that its limits are well defined: 1 and 0. As a consequence, it may be interpreted at the interval level.

We have applied Yasuda's index and the $M_B$ index to data presented by Jackson and Crockett (1964). These data deal with three American mobility studies conducted in 1947, 1952 and 1957. Considering only the exchanges between manual and non-

28

manual workers, Yasuda's mobility index yields 0.55, 0.61 and 0.57, respectively, for the three periods. This would suggest an oscillatory movement in the mobility process if Yasuda's index could be interpreted at the interval level. We have already alluded to this example and saw that it could not be so considered. The values of the mobility index $M_B$ are, on the other hand, respectively 0.26, 0.33 and 0.32 for the three periods. Here, the values can be interpreted at the interval level and appear to indicate an increasing trend of the mobility process, even if the amount of mobility decreases slightly between 1952 and 1957. Of course, drawing firm conclusions from the consideration of three time periods is very dangerous. But the example is aimed simply at illustrating the comparison between $M_B$ and $M_Y$.

*The generalization of $I_B$ to polytomies*

The generalization of $I_B$ to polytomies is easier than the generalization of Yasuda's index. As we recall, the generalization of $I_Y$ proposed by Yasuda may be described as ad hoc: by contrast with the dichotomous index, the polytomous generalization has no clear meaning, except that it derives from an averaging process. This does not imply that it should not be useful in practice, but only that it may be dangerous: in some cases, it may be misleading to summarize the structure of a polytomous mobility table by a single index. However, Yasuda's polytomous index may be computed in every case, whether it is reasonable or not to summarize by a single index a polytomous structure containing several degrees of freedom.

A similar generalization can easily be derived for $I_B$ by averaging each term of the dichotomous formula. Let us call $I_B{}^G$ this generalization.

$$I_B{}^G = \frac{\sum\limits_i n_{ii} - \sum\limits_i (n_{.i} - n_{\bar{i}.})*}{\sum\limits_i \min(n_{i.}, n_{.i}) - \sum\limits_i (n_{.i} - n_{\bar{i}.})*} \tag{1.44}$$

This formula is directly derived from eqn. (1.29). The summation extends from $i = 1$ to $i = \sigma$, while $n_{\bar{i}}$ stands for the number of people in the first generation who are not $i$, *i.e.* who are 1, 2, ..., $(i - 1)$, $(i + 1)$, ..., $\sigma$.

Let us compute $I_B{}^G$ for the example of Table 1.11.

TABLE 1.11

A fictitious trichotomous turnover mobility table

| Father's social status | Son's social status | | | |
|---|---|---|---|---|
| | 1 | 2 | 3 | |
| 1 | 172 | 88 | 40 | 300 |
| 2 | 8 | 32 | 160 | 200 |
| 3 | 20 | 80 | 400 | 500 |
| | 200 | 200 | 600 | 1000 |

Taking successively $i$ = 1, 2 and 3 and applying eqn. (1.44)

$$I_B^G = \frac{(172 + 32 + 400) - (0 + 0 + 100)}{(200 + 200 + 500) - (0 + 0 + 100)} = 0.63$$

Using eqn. (1.39), it may easily be verified that $I_B^G$ is equal to $I_B$ when $\sigma = 2$. However, $I_B^G$ is again an ad hoc measure *. It is certainly more interesting to try, step by step, to extend to poly-tomies the general rationale which led us to $I_B$, rather than to generalize directly by averaging.

Let us consider the matrix of Table 1.11 as compared with the matrices of Tables 1.12 and 1.13, which have the same marginals, but are otherwise different from one another. The matrix of

TABLE 1.12

A turnover matrix with two degrees of freedom

| Father's social status | Son's social status | | | |
|---|---|---|---|---|
| | 1 | 2 | 3 | |
| 1 | 144 | 116 | 40 | 300 |
| 2 | 16 | 24 | 160 | 200 |
| 3 | 40 | 60 | 400 | 500 |
| | 200 | 200 | 600 | 1000 |

Table 1.11 has an interesting structure which may be described as follows.

---

* An interpretation of this measure will, however, be given below; see eqn. (1.64).

TABLE 1.13

A turnover matrix with four degrees of freedom

| Father's social status | Son's social status | | | |
|---|---|---|---|---|
| | 1 | 2 | 3 | |
| 1 | 130 | 90 | 80 | 300 |
| 2 | 40 | 40 | 120 | 200 |
| 3 | 30 | 70 | 400 | 500 |
| | 200 | 200 | 600 | 1000 |

$$n_{33} = x \min(n_{3.}, n_{.3}) \tag{1.45a}$$

$$n_{23} = x \min(n_{2.}, n_{.3} - n_{33}) \tag{1.45b}$$

$$n_{32} = x \min(n_{.2}, n_{3.} - n_{33}) \tag{1.45c}$$

$$n_{22} = x \min(n_{2.} - n_{23}, n_{.2} - n_{32}) \tag{1.45d}$$

with $x = 0.80$. Indeed, taking this value for $x$ and using eqns. (1.45), we reproduce the figures in Table 1.11.

By contrast, the structure of Table 1.12 is

$$n_{33} = x_1 \min(n_{3.}, n_{.3}) \tag{1.46a}$$

$$n_{23} = x_1 \min(n_{2.}, n_{.3} - n_{33}) \tag{1.46b}$$

$$n_{32} = x_2 \min(n_{.2}, n_{3.} - n_{33}) \tag{1.46c}$$

$$n_{22} = x_2 \min(n_{2.} - n_{23}, n_{.2} - n_{32}) \tag{1.46d}$$

with $x_1 = 0.80$ and $x_2 = 0.60$.

Finally, the structure of Table 1.13 is described by

$$n_{33} = x_1 \min(n_{3.}, n_{.3}) \tag{1.47a}$$

$$n_{23} = x_2 \min(n_{2.}, n_{.3} - n_{33}) \tag{1.47b}$$

$$n_{32} = x_3 \min(n_{.2}, n_{3.} - n_{33}) \tag{1.47c}$$

$$n_{22} = x_4 \min(n_{2.} - n_{23}, n_{.2} - n_{32}) \tag{1.47d}$$

with $x_1 = 0.80$, $x_2 = 0.60$, $x_3 = 0.70$ and $x_4 = 0.50$.

31

We may summarize these structural differences by saying Table 1.11 is a matrix with one degree of freedom (of type $D_1$), Table 1.12 a matrix with two degrees of freedom (type $D_2$) and Table 1.13 a matrix with four degrees of freedom (type $D_4$). With $\sigma$ strata, the maximum number of degrees of freedom is, of course, $(\sigma - 1)(\sigma - 1)$.

The interpretation of these degrees of freedom is straightforward. Let us return to our fictitious decision maker (DM) ruling over the mobility process. For $D_1$ matrices, DM chooses a single value for $x$, without making any distinctions between origin—destination categories. In the $D_2$ matrix of Table 1.12, DM adds to his general rule of restraining mobility a further difference in favor of the destination category 3. In the $D_4$ matrix of Table 1.13, he makes a differential choice for each origin—destination category.

One of the consequences of this analysis is that we have to distinguish between $D_1$ and not-$D_1$ matrices. If we want to generalize the rationale for $I_B$ to polytomies we should take into account the following.

(1) If a matrix is $D_1$ (or close to a $D_1$ matrix), then it is not difficult to construct a generalized index following the same rationale as for the dichotomous index $I_B$.

(2) If a polytomous matrix is not $D_1$, then it is questionable whether trying to build an overall mobility index is at all reasonable.

It must, however, be noted that a matrix is $D_1$, $D_2$, etc., not absolutely, but with respect to a given ordering of the social categories. Let us, for instance, suppose that DM chooses to fill the matrix 1.11 starting from the upper left corner rather than from the lower right one. Then, the structure of this matrix would have to be represented by four parameters rather than by one. In other words, the matrix 1.11 is $D_1$ if, and only if, we accept the model according to which DM would fill the matrix using the order 3,2,1.

Thus, let us consider exclusively $D_1$ matrices. We shall call $I_B{}^H$ the extension of $I_B$ to polytomous $D_1$ matrices. Of course

$$I_B{}^H = \frac{x - x_{min}}{1 - x_{min}} \qquad (1.48)$$

The determination of $x$ does not raise any problem. Its definition is given by eqn. (1.45). However, the computation of $x_{min}$ is much more complicated in the polytomous case.

Whatever the order of a matrix, it is easily verified that, if $x$ is defined by eqn. (1.45), $x_{min}$ is the value of $x$ which leads to

$$n_{11} = 0 \qquad (1.49)$$

The next step is to find an expression for $n_{11}$ which contains exclusively the quantities appearing in eqn. (1.45). If we take the trichotomous case, this is readily accomplished. We have, for instance

$$n_{11} = n_{.1} - n_{31} - n_{21}$$

$$= n_{.1} - n_{3.} - n_{2.} + n_{33} + n_{23} + n_{32} + n_{22} \qquad (1.50)$$

Therefore, using eqns. (1.45)

$$n_{11} = n_{.1} - n_{3.} - n_{2.} + x[\min(n_{3.}, n_{.3}) + \min(n_{2.}, n_{.3} - n_{33})$$

$$+ \min(n_{.2}, n_{3.} - n_{33}) + \min(n_{2.} - n_{23}, n_{.2} - n_{32})] \qquad (1.51)$$

Obviously, eqn. (1.51) cannot, in this form, be solved for $x$, since some of the terms in brackets are a function of $x$, as can be seen from eqns. (1.45). Then, the next step is to look for the ranges of $x$ corresponding to the possible specifications of eqn. (1.51). Let us take, for instance, the case of Table 1.11. One of these ranges, say $A_1$, is defined by*

$$0 \leqslant x \leqslant 0.60 \qquad (1.52)$$

Indeed, when $x$ takes values within these limits, the marginals of Table 1.11 are such that eqns. (1.45) are specified into

$$n_{33} = xn_{3.} \qquad (1.53a)$$

$$n_{23} = xn_{2.} \qquad (1.53b)$$

$$n_{32} = xn_{.2} \qquad (1.53c)$$

$$n_{22} = x(n_{2.} - n_{23}) = x(n_{2.} - xn_{2.}) \qquad (1.53d)$$

The following range, say $A_2$, is defined by the limits

$$0.60 \leqslant x \leqslant 0.80 \qquad (1.54)$$

In this range, eqns. (1.45) are specified by

---

* The general method for the determination of these ranges is given in Chapter 4, Section 4.3.

$$n_{33.} = xn_{3.} \tag{1.55a}$$

$$n_{23} = xn_{2.} \tag{1.55b}$$

$$n_{32} = x(n_{3.} - n_{33}) = x(n_{3.} - xn_{3.}) \tag{1.55c}$$

$$n_{22} = x(n_{2.} - n_{23}) = x(n_{2.} - xn_{2.}) \tag{1.55d}$$

Since $x$=0.80 for Table 1.11, it is not necessary to look for the ranges of $x$ such that $x_{min}$ is greater than 0.80. Let us now take the first range $A_1$. In this range, eqns. (1.45) are specified by eqns. (1.53). Then, we substitute eqns. (1.53) in eqns. (1.50), in order to obtain for $n_{11}$ an expression replacing eqn. (1.51) and including exclusively $x$ and the marginals.

$$n_{11} = n_{.1} - n_{3.} - n_{2.} + xn_{3.} + xn_{2.} + xn_{.2} + x(n_{2.} - xn_{2.})$$

$$= n_{.1} - n_{3.} - n_{2.} + x(n_{3.} + 2n_{2.} + n_{.2}) - x^2 n_{2.} \tag{1.56}$$

Substituting the empirical figures drawn from Table 1.11 into eqn. (1.56) and putting $n_{11} = 0$, we obtain the quadratic equation

$$0 = -500 + 1100x - 200x^2 \tag{1.57}$$

the roots of which are 5 and 0.50. The former is, of course, inapplicable, since $x_{min}$ is a proportion between 0 and 1. The latter is acceptable, since it is located within the bounds of the area $A_1$ defined by eqn. (1.52). Then

$$x_{min} = 0.50 \tag{1.58}$$

It is readily verified that this figure actually generates $n_{11} = 0$ when eqn. (1.45) is applied to the marginals of Table 1.11.

Of course, if eqn. (1.56) had no roots within the bounds limiting range $A_1$, we would have had to move to area $A_2$, $i.e.$

(1) substitute eqns. (1.55) into eqn. (1.50);
(2) set $n_{11} = 0$;
(3) solve the resulting equation; and
(4) take the minimal real root included in the variation bounds of $A_2$ as the value of $x_{min}$.

In summary, the procedure for determining the value of $x_{min}$ is the following

34

(1) write the specification of eqn. (1.45) in $A_1$, introduce this specification into eqn. (1.50) and set $n_{11} = 0$;

(2) look for the bounds of $A_1$;

(3) solve the equation resulting from (1) to see if it has a root within the bounds of $A_1$;

(4) if so, take this root as the value of $x_{min}$;

(5) if not, start the procedure over again with the next range $A_2$.

Finally, the value of the immobility index for Table 1.11 is

$$I_B^H = \frac{0.80 - 0.50}{1 - 0.50} = 0.60 \tag{1.59}$$

This value is not very far from the value given by the ad hoc index $I_B^G$ (0.63). However, as expected, it is not identical.

The procedure for determining $I_B^H$ which has been illustrated in the case of a trichotomy may, of course, be extended to a matrix of any order, provided it has (at least almost) a $D_1$ structure, i.e. that it may reasonably be described by a single parameter. The practical determination of $x_{min}$, however, becomes more complicated as the order of the matrix increases. But this problem may be easily solved by using an iterative computer program.

## 1.5. Counting indices

Of course, many other indices can be, or have actually been, defined. Gabor and Gabor (1954, 1955, 1958) and McFarland (1969) have proposed very interesting indices using the language of information theory.

An index, suggested by the work of Kahl (1957), and formalized by Matras (1961), is also worth mentioning. This index uses the distinction between pure (or exchange) mobility and structural mobility, as do $I_Y$ and $I_B$. But an important distinction exists between these indices and the Matras index: as we saw, $I_Y$ and $I_B$ are essentially defined for dichotomies; their extension to polytomies is either ad hoc or supposes that restrictive conditions are met. By contrast, the Matras index is directly defined for polytomies. This advantage is, however, counterbalanced by the fact that the index is simply a counting measure, the conceptual elaboration of which is much less sophisticated than that of the previously presented indices.

Let us define $M_{\mathrm{M}}$ as

$$M_{\mathrm{M}} = \frac{\text{total mobility} - \text{structural mobility}}{\text{total mobility}} \tag{1.60}$$

$M_{\mathrm{M}}$ describes, in other words, the proportion of exchange or pure mobiles to total number of mobiles. Formally, the definitions are the following.

(1) Total mobility $= N - \sum_i n_{ii}$

(2) Structural mobility $= N - \sum_i \min(n_{i.}, n_{.i})$

Then

$$M_{\mathrm{M}} = \frac{(N - \sum_i n_{ii}) - [N - \sum_i \min(n_{i.}, n_{.i})]}{N - \sum_i n_{ii}}$$

$$= \frac{\sum_i \min(n_{i.}, n_{.i}) - \sum_i n_{ii}}{N - \sum_i n_{ii}} \tag{1.61}$$

Of course, a complementary immobility index is defined by $1 - M_{\mathrm{M}}$. This index has the advantage that it can be immediately defined on polytomies. Matras has applied it to some of the data presented by Lipset and Bendix (1960). He shows that, while total mobility is very different from one country to another, the proportion of exchange mobility is almost the same in the United States, France, Germany, Japan, etc. As we recall, a different picture was drawn from the application of Yasuda's index. This is not surprising, since the Matras index measures the proportion of the mobility which is not structural rather than the amount of non-structural mobility. Thus, the value of the index may be very high even if the amount of this exchange or non-structural mobility is low.

This suggests a variation of the Matras index in which exchange mobility is referred, not to total mobility but rather to the maximum amount of exchange mobility which is possible, given the marginals. Let us call this index $M_{\mathrm{S}}$. Its formulation is

36

$$M_S = \frac{\text{total mobility} - \text{structural mobility}}{\text{maximum mobility} - \text{structural mobility}} \qquad (1.62)$$

Structural mobility is defined, as in the case of the Matras, of the Yasuda and of the $M_B$ index, as the minimum number of mobiles determined by the marginals. This structural mobility can also be called a minimum mobility. Maximum mobility, on the other hand, would be the maximum number of movers determined by the marginals. Formally, it is readily verified

that total mobility is $N - \sum_i n_{ii}$

that structural (minimum) mobility is $N - \sum_i \min(n_{i.}, n_{.i})$

and that maximum mobility is $N - \sum_i (n_{i.} - n_{.\bar{i}})*$

In this latter formula, the notation is the same as in eqn. (1.44): $n_{.\bar{i}}$ stands for the sum

$$n_{.1} + n_{.2} + \ldots + n_{.(1-1)} + n_{.(1+1)} + \ldots + n_{.\sigma}$$

(in the case of $\sigma$ strata) and the asterisk (*) indicates that the difference is made equal to zero if

$$n_{i.} - n_{.\bar{i}} \leqslant 0 \qquad (1.63)$$

Then

$$
\begin{aligned}
M_S &= \frac{(N - \sum_i n_{ii}) - [N - \sum_i \min(n_{i.}, n_{.i})]}{N - \sum_i (n_{i.} - n_{.\bar{i}})* - [N - \sum_i \min(n_{i.}, n_{.i})]} \\
&= \frac{\sum_i \min(n_{i.}, n_{.i}) - \sum_i n_{ii}}{\sum_i \min(n_{i.}, n_{.i}) - \sum_i (n_{i.} - n_{.\bar{i}})*} \qquad (1.64)
\end{aligned}
$$

The rationale for this index is obvious: the number of exchange mobiles is measured, using as a base the difference between the maximum and the minimum number of mobiles determined by the marginals. Another way to describe this index would be to say that it measures the proportion of the maximum possible amount of pure (exchange) mobility which actually occurs in a society.

Let us finally note that maximum mobility can alternatively be expressed by

$$N - \sum_i (n_{.i} - n_{j.})*$$

Then, the immobility index corresponding to $M_S$ is

$$I_S = 1 - M_S$$

$$= \frac{\sum_i n_{ii} - \sum_i (n_{.i} - n_{\bar{i}.})*}{\sum_i \min(n_{i.}, n_{.i}) - \sum_i (n_{.i} - n_{\bar{i}.})*} \qquad (1.65)$$

Since eqn. (1.65) is the same as eqn. (1.44), $I_S$ is an interpretation of $I_B{}^G$, the ad hoc generalization of $I_B$.

In order to visualize the difference between the Matras index, $M_M$ and $M_S$, let us imagine two societies in which the minimum and the actual numbers of mobiles are the same, but where the maximum number of mobiles is different (Fig. 1.1). Both are characterized by the same $M_M$ index. But they are different from the point of view of $M_S$. Conversely, if we suppose, for instance, that the actual number of mobiles in the second society is 1250 instead of 750 and if we retain the other figures, the two $M_M$ indices will be different, while the $M_S$ indices will be the same.

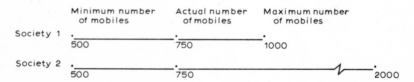

Fig. 1.1. Situation in which the indices $M_M$ are equal for two societies, while the indices $M_S$ are different.

It would be possible to introduce still other indices. But we prefer at this point to refer the reader to the literature*, since our main aim in this review is to show that, while some indices cannot be used without caution because of their logical weaknesses, there is no unique best index of mobility. The last one considered, $M_S$, belongs to the category of counting indices: it compares the actual number to the maximum possible number of exchange mobiles. Its

---

* See, for instance, Billewicz (1955), Capecchi (1967), Goodman (1969), Levine (1967), etc.

ease of application to polytomous tables certainly makes it a useful mobility index.

Yasuda's index, as well as the $I_B$ index both belong to another category, that of structural indices, as we have called them. Both suppose, in order to be adequately extended to polytomies, a specific structure of the mobility matrix. We have examined this point in detail in the case of $I_B$. This disadvantage is counterbalanced by the fact that the structural indices are more satisfactory from a conceptual point of view. Indeed, both $I_B$ and $I_Y$ derive, or may be considered as deriving from, a theory. $I_B$ may be considered as a measure of the discrimination factor which rules over the distribution of the individuals in the social classes. But $I_Y$ can also be given the same meaning, since, as we recall, the structure of the two indices is the same.

Finally, and this is perhaps the most important point which emerges from this review, the problem of choosing a mobility index is not a purely logical and mathematical one. It is also, one might say, a semantic one. If we choose to understand by mobility a pure physical movement, *i.e.* if we are only interested in the amount of movement, without caring about the social character of this movement, $M_M$ and preferably $M_S$ are very adequate indices. But is this what we want? In fact, when we speak of pure or exchange mobility in relation to indices $M_M$ or $M_S$, this should not, strictly speaking, be interpreted as meaning more than "mobility not accounted for by changes in the social structure". But the concept of pure mobility is often interpreted as meaning more, *i.e.* as being an indicator of the freedom of the individuals within the social structures. For this reason, structural indices are probably preferable to counting indices.

This review also shows that mobility indices always include implicit or explicit assumptions. Mobility may or may not be considered as dependent on the changes in the social structures. The reference point may be perfect or maximum mobility. Finally, some indices derive from theories. The index $I_B$, which formalizes the assumption that the individuals are distributed in social categories according to an inequalitarian allocation process, belongs to this category.

CHAPTER 2

# Measures Derived from Mathematical Models: Structural Analysis of Mobility Matrices

## 2.1. Introductory remarks

In the previous chapter, we have dealt with indices all more or less directly derived from the concept of mobility. In the present chapter, we shall consider measures which are somewhat more sophisticated in the sense that they are derived from mathematical models.

These models are, for the most part, Markov chains. However, we shall also meet models which, although inspired by Markov chain theory, are not actually Markov chains. Sections 2.2 and 2.3 will deal with measures using Markov chain models, Section 2.4 with a family of models using a more complicated approach.

On the other hand, we shall deal in Section 2.5 with tools which may be considered as functional substitutes for indices. They are used when the association of a single index with a mobility matrix does not seem reasonable or possible. An index is used to permit a comparison between matrices. When summarization of the structure of the matrices by indices does not seem desirable, comparison may still be possible. An adequate set of parameters may be defined and this set used for comparison. Or, alternatively, one of the matrices to be compared may be selected as pivotal and the others transformed in an appropriate way so that they all have the same marginals.

Let us also note that some of the concepts and models introduced in Section 2.4 will be referred to again in the theoretical second part of this book.

## 2.2. A first mobility index using Markov chains

In the previous chapter, we used exclusively turnover matrices. As we recall, a turnover matrix is a table giving the number (or the proportion) of people who are $i$ at one time and $j$ at the following time unit, $e.g.$ people who have social origin $i$ (status of their father) and current status $j$. The elements $n_{ij}$ of a turnover matrix add up to $N$, the size of the population. If the proportions $p_{ij}$ are used instead of the numbers $n_{ij}$, the overall sum is of course 1.

In the following, we shall primarily use transition matrices. Let $r_{ij}$ be an element of a transition matrix. It describes the proportion of people who are $j$ at a given time, among those who were $i$ at the previous time or, in the language of probabilities, the conditional probability of going to state $j$ from state $i$. By contrast, the element $p_{ij}$ of a turnover matrix of proportions describes the proportion of people who were $i$ and who are $j$. As a consequence of the definition of $r_{ij}$

$$\sum_j r_{ij} = 1 \qquad (2.1)$$

In other words, the row totals of a transition matrix are each equal to 1.

Of course, transition and turnover matrices are related to one another. For instance, let $\mathbf{P}$ be a turnover matrix of proportions with $\mathbf{R}$ the corresponding transition matrix and let $\mathbf{D}$ be a diagonal matrix, the elements of which are the row totals of $\mathbf{P}$

$$p_1., p_2., ..., p_\sigma.$$

Then, it is easily verified that

$$\mathbf{P} = \mathbf{DR} \qquad (2.2)$$

*Markov chains applied to mobility analysis*

Transition matrices are a basic concept of Markov chain theory\*. Since a turnover mobility matrix can, using eqn. (2.2), be

---

\* See, for instance, on Markov Chain Theory, Bartlett (1955), Feller (1950, 1965), Hajnal (1956, 1958), Karlin (1968), Kemeny et al. (1957, 1960).

changed into a transition matrix, the idea of applying Markov chain theory to mobility is very natural. However, we shall see later that Markov chains, when directly applied to the analysis of mobility tables, do not lead to very satisfactory results. More refined models are needed, but the simple applications of Markov chains we are going to describe in this section undoubtedly played an important role in the development of a mathematically oriented research tradition in the field of mobility.

Although the use of Markov chains is certainly widespread, it may be useful to summarize briefly some basic concepts and results of Markov chain theory.

Since the applications of this theory will lead us to consider, not only two generations as in the previous chapter, but more, we shall have to modify the notation previously used. In Chapter 1, the proportions of fathers belonging respectively to social strata 1, 2, ..., $\sigma$ and were described by

$$p_1, p_2, \ldots, p_\sigma.$$

while the corresponding proportions for the sons were

$$p_{.1}, p_{.2}, \ldots, p_{.\sigma}$$

By contrast, we shall now associate the numbers 0, 1, 2, etc. with a sequence of generations and describe the distributions at each of these successive generations by

$$p_{(0)1}, p_{(0)2}, \ldots, p_{(0)\sigma}$$
$$p_{(1)1}, p_{(1)2}, \ldots, p_{(1)\sigma}$$
$$p_{(2)1}, p_{(2)2}, \ldots, p_{(2)\sigma}$$
etc.

Then, the proportions of fathers belonging respectively to social strata 1, 2, ..., $\sigma$, are described by

$$p_{(0)1}, p_{(0)2}, \ldots, p_{(0)\sigma}$$

yielding the row vector

$$\mathbf{p}_0 = [p_{(0)i}] \tag{2.3}$$

Also, the proportions of sons are described by

$$p_{(1)1}, p_{(1)2}, \ldots, p_{(1)\sigma}$$

with corresponding row vector

$$\mathbf{p}_1 = [p_{(1)i}] \qquad\qquad (2.4)$$

Finally,

$$\mathbf{R} = [r_{ij}] \qquad\qquad (2.5)$$

is the transition matrix derived from a mobility turnover matrix using eqn. (2.2).

Then it is readily verified that

$$[p_{(0)1} \ p_{(0)2} \ \cdots \ p_{(0)\sigma}] \begin{bmatrix} r_{11} & r_{12} & \cdots & r_{1\sigma} \\ r_{21} & r_{22} & \cdots & r_{2\sigma} \\ r_{\sigma 1} & r_{\sigma 2} & \cdots & r_{\sigma\sigma} \end{bmatrix} = [p_{(1)1} \ p_{(1)2} \ \cdots \ p_{(1)\sigma}]$$

$$(2.6a)$$

or, in matrix form,

$$\mathbf{p}_0 \mathbf{R} = \mathbf{p}_1 \qquad\qquad (2.6b)$$

It should be noted that eqns. (2.6a) and (2.6b) are tautological *i.e.* that these equations do not incorporate any specific assumptions.

Let us now go further and assume that the empirical transition matrix $\mathbf{R}$ observed at a given time describes the transition rates not only at this particular time, but also at future times. Let us assume, in other words, that $\mathbf{R}$ may be considered as stable over an extended period of time. To begin with, let us suppose that the sons whose occupational distribution is described by the row vector $\mathbf{p}_1$ will in turn have sons distributed in the social categories according to the transition rules of $\mathbf{R}$. Let us call $\mathbf{p}_2$ the occupational distribution at the third generation, then

$$\mathbf{p}_2 = \mathbf{p}_1 \mathbf{R} \qquad\qquad (2.7)$$

or, substituting eqn. (2.6) into eqn. (2.7)

$$\mathbf{p}_2 = \mathbf{p}_0 \mathbf{R}^2 \qquad\qquad (2.8)$$

In the same way, we have, for the fourth generation

$$\mathbf{p}_3 = \mathbf{p}_2 \mathbf{R} = \mathbf{p}_0 \mathbf{R}^3 \qquad\qquad (2.9)$$

and generally, at the $(t+1)$th generation

$$\mathbf{p}_t = \mathbf{p}_{(t-1)} \mathbf{R} = \mathbf{p}_0 \mathbf{R}^t \qquad\qquad (2.10)$$

Of course, the assumption of stability of $\mathbf{R}$ over several generations is not very realistic. Thus eqn. (2.10) would be purely a speculative result without the existence of an important theorem in the theory of Markov chains which states that, as $t$ increases, at a limit, a further multiplication of the input vector $\mathbf{p}_t$ by $\mathbf{R}$ does not modify the distribution. Formally, for large $t$

$$\mathbf{p}_{(t-1)}\mathbf{R} \sim \mathbf{p}_{(t-1)} \tag{2.11}$$

Thus, since

$$\mathbf{p}_t = \mathbf{p}_{(t-1)}\mathbf{R}$$

$$\mathbf{p}_t \sim \mathbf{p}_{(t-1)} \tag{2.12}$$

for large $t$.

On the other hand, it may be shown that under broad conditions ($\mathbf{R}$ **positive** or any power of $\mathbf{R}$ positive), $\mathbf{R}^t$ converges. In other words, for large $t$

$$\mathbf{R}^t \sim \mathbf{R}^{(t-1)} \tag{2.13}$$

(In the following we shall always consider that $\mathbf{R}$ is positive.) Thus, in the limit, $\mathbf{p}_t$ will reach an equilibrium value, say $\mathbf{p}^*$, and $\mathbf{R}^t$ will also reach an equilibrium value, say $\mathbf{R}^*$. This may be summarized by

$$\mathbf{p}^* = \mathbf{p}^*\mathbf{R}^* \tag{2.14}$$

The equilibrium matrix $\mathbf{R}^*$ will be a matrix with all rows equal.

One may, of course, wonder if theorem (2.14) is useful for intergenerational mobility studies in which the time unit is one generation. Even if the equilibrium stage is reached for a moderate value of $t$, this value can correspond to a rather long time and the assumption of stability of $\mathbf{R}$ even for, say, three or four generations may be very unrealistic. But eqn. (2.14) may be given another interpretation. The equilibrium distribution $\mathbf{p}^*$ may be interpreted, not as a prediction of what should actually occur in the more or less remote future, but rather as a way of summarizing the structure of $\mathbf{R}$, the empirical transition matrix observed at a given present time. This is so because $\mathbf{p}^*$ depends only on $\mathbf{R}$ and not on $\mathbf{p}_0$. In most applications of eqn. (2.14) to intergenerational mobility, $\mathbf{p}^*$ is, in fact, given this latter meaning: it is interpreted less as a prediction of a future state of affairs than as a structural characteristic of $\mathbf{R}$, the empirical transition matrix.

We shall now consider two examples in which eqn. (2.14) is used to define a mobility index.

## The Prais index: a reformulation using Markov chains without the equilibrium distribution

The first example is borrowed from the pioneering work of Prais (1955a and b). It is worth reviewing, since Prais was probably the first author to apply Markov chain theory to social mobility. His research was inspired by the work of Glass and his colleagues (1954) on social mobility in Britain. Prais' confidence in Markov chain theory applied to mobility was corroborated by the fact that the equilibrium distribution $\mathbf{p}*$ derived from the empirical intergenerational matrix $\mathbf{R}$ which Glass observed in Britain is not very different from $\mathbf{p}_1$, the actual distribution of Glass' respondents.

Prais first had the interesting idea of applying Markov chains in order to determine the average number of generations a family is likely to spend in a given occupational stratum. This can, of course, only be done by supposing $\mathbf{R}$ stable through time. But again, it is not necessary to give this variable a predictive interpretation. Prais' idea was rather to use this expected number of generations spent in each social stratum as an indicator of, say, the degree of status inheritance characterizing, hic et nunc, the various social strata.

Consider the families belonging to, say, social category $i$. Among them, a proportion $r_{ii}$ will remain in the same category at the next generation, while a proportion $(1 - r_{ii})$ will move to other social strata. In other words, a proportion $(1 - r_{ii})$ will remain in category $i$ exactly one generation. (Note that this statement and the following introduce implicitly the assumption of the absence of differential fertility since they assume that each father gives birth to exactly one son; we shall ignore this point for the moment since Markov chain theory is used here for analyzing the structure of the empirical matrix $\mathbf{R}$ rather than for predictive purposes.)

Families remaining in a social stratum for exactly two generations must stay there two generations and then leave. Thus, the probability for a family to stay two generations in the same stratum is $r_{ii}(1 - r_{ii})$. In the same way, the probabilities for a family to stay in the same social category exactly 3, 4, etc. generations will be respectively

$$r_{ii}^2(1 - r_{ii}) , \qquad r_{ii}^3(1 - r_{ii}) , \qquad \text{etc.}$$

Weighting these quantities according to the number of generations, we obtain the average number of generations during which a family may expect to stay in the same social stratum. Let us call $v_i$ this number for stratum $i$.

$$v_i = 1 \times (1 - r_{ii}) + 2 \times r_{ii}(1 - r_{ii})$$

$$+ 3 \times r_{ii}^2(1 - r_{ii}) + 4 \times r_{ii}^3(1 - r_{ii}) + ... \tag{2.15}$$

It is readily verified that

$$v_i = 1 + r_{ii} + r_{ii}^2 + r_{ii}^3 + ... \tag{2.16}$$

Thus, $v_i$ is the sum of the elements of a geometrical series with $r_{ii} < 1$, so that

$$v_i = \frac{1}{1 - r_{ii}} \tag{2.17}$$

Let us suppose, as usual, $\sigma$ social categories and call $\mathbf{v}$ the vector

$$[v_1 \ v_2 \ ... \ v_\sigma] = [v_i] \tag{2.18}$$

This vector, which may be very easily computed from the matrix $\mathbf{R}$ using eqn. (2.17), may be considered as a useful characterization of $\mathbf{R}$. Indeed, it provides a set of differential measures of social inheritance within a given society.

In order to use this measure for intersocietal comparisons, it is necessary to eliminate the effects on $\mathbf{v}$ of the marginals of the turnover matrix $\mathbf{P}$ corresponding to the transition matrix $\mathbf{R}$. A slightly modified version of the device suggested by Prais (and directly inspired by Glass' work) consists in comparing $\mathbf{v}$ with the vector $\mathbf{v}^{**}$ which we obtain under the assumption of perfect mobility. More precisely, let us construct a diagonal matrix

$$\mathbf{D}_0 = \text{diag}[p_{(0)i}] \tag{2.19}$$

including the proportions of fathers belonging respectively to social categories 1, 2, ..., $\sigma$. Then

$$\mathbf{D}_0\mathbf{R} = \mathbf{P} \tag{2.20}$$

with $\mathbf{P}$ the turnover matrix of proportions corresponding to $\mathbf{R}$. Let us now call $\mathbf{P}^{**}$ a proportion turnover matrix with the same marginals as $\mathbf{P}$ but characterized by perfect mobility. Then

$$\mathbf{P}^{**} = [p_{ij}^{**}] = [p_{(0)i} \cdot p_{(1)j}] \tag{2.21}$$

Next, premultiply $\mathbf{P}^{**}$ by the inverse, $\mathbf{D}_0^{-1}$, of $\mathbf{D}_0$ in order to transform it into a transition matrix and call the result $\mathbf{R}^{**}$.

$$
\mathbf{D_0}^{-1}\mathbf{P}^{**} = \begin{bmatrix} p_{(1)1} & p_{(1)2} & \cdots p_{(1)\sigma} \\ p_{(1)1} & p_{(1)2} & \cdots p_{(1)\sigma} \\ \cdots\cdots\cdots\cdots\cdots\cdots\cdots \\ p_{(1)1} & p_{(1)2} & \cdots p_{(1)\sigma} \end{bmatrix} = \mathbf{R}^{**} \tag{2.22}
$$

As we see here, the perfect mobility assumption is translated by the fact that the transition matrix $\mathbf{R}^{**}$ has its rows all equal. This was, of course, expected since, in the case of perfect mobility, the probability of going to a given social status is the same whatever the origin category. Thus $\mathbf{R}^{**}$ is the perfect mobility version of $\mathbf{R}$ in the sense that it is the perfect mobility matrix derived from the marginals of $\mathbf{P}$.

Hence arises the idea (again, a slightly modified version of Prais' original procedure) of using, as an index of mobility, the ratio of the elements of $\mathbf{v}$ to the elements of $\mathbf{v}^{**}$, the vector giving the lengths of time spent in the various social strata when the transition matrix is $\mathbf{R}^{**}$ rather than $\mathbf{R}$.

Let $v_i^{**}$ be an element of $\mathbf{v}^{**}$. A derivation similar to eqn. (2.15) to eqn. (2.17) leads to

$$
v_i^{**} = \frac{1}{1 - p_{(1)i}} \tag{2.23}
$$

since the $(i, i)$th element of $\mathbf{R}^{**}$ is $p_{(1)i}$.

Let us now call $w_i^{**}$ the ratio of $v_i$ to $v_i^{**}$. This ratio describes the length of stay in stratum $i$, taking as a measurement unit the length of stay in stratum $i$ which would be observed under the assumption of perfect mobility. Apparently, this index is acceptable for intersocietal comparisons, since $\mathbf{v}^{**}$ is derived from the marginals of $\mathbf{P}$. Thus dividing $v_i$ by $v_i^{**}$ seems to make possible a comparison of turnover matrices with different marginals. Let us, however, look more closely at this index.

$$
w_i^{**} = \frac{v_i}{v_i^{**}} = \frac{1/(1 - r_{ii})}{1/(1 - p_{(1)i})} = \frac{1 - p_{(1)i}}{1 - r_{ii}} \tag{2.24}
$$

As we recall

$$r_{ii} = \frac{p_{ii}}{p_{(0)i}}$$ (2.25)

so that

$$w_i^{**} = \frac{1 - p_{(1)i}}{1 - p_{ii}/p_{(0)i}} = \frac{p_{(0)i}(1 - p_{(1)i})}{p_{(0)i} - p_{ii}}$$ (2.26)

In the notation of Chapter 1

$$w_i^{**} = \frac{p_{i.}(1 - p_{.i})}{p_{i.} - p_{ii}}$$ (2.27)

This is simply the reciprocal of the Glass mobility index defined by eqn. (1.14). Now we recall the objections which were raised to this index. Principally it is not really independent of the marginals of the turnover matrix. The reason why we return to the same weakness and even to the same index is that, although $\mathbf{R}^{**}$ derives from the marginals of $\mathbf{P}^{**}$, the marginals are not actually accounted for, $\mathbf{R}^{**}$ being a transition matrix.

*Prais' original index*

The interest of eqn. (2.27) is purely speculative: it gives an interesting interpretation of the Glass index in terms of expected duration of stay in a social category. On the other hand, this slightly modified reformulation of Prais' index has the advantage of showing more clearly the basic structure of the original index.

The difference between the reformulation which has just been expounded and the original index proposed by Prais is that the latter uses $\mathbf{R}^*$ instead of $\mathbf{R}^{**}$. As we recall, $\mathbf{R}^{**}$ is the perfect mobility matrix derived from $\mathbf{R}$, while $\mathbf{R}^*$ is, by eqn. (2.14), the equilibrium matrix, $\lim \mathbf{R}^t$.

Now, since $\mathbf{R}^*$ is a matrix with all rows equal, it is also a perfect mobility matrix. On the other hand, as we recall, in the data considered by Prais, the distribution of the respondents is very close to the equilibrium distribution. In many cases, the Prais index should not be very different from the Glass index. And even if they are different, they should lead to closely related interpretations since they are structurally similar.

The numerator of the Prais index is, of course, the same as the numerator of the reformulated index described by eqn. (2.17). Let us call the denominator $v_i*$. A derivation similar to eqn. (2.15) and to eqn. (2.17) shows that

$$v_i* = \frac{1}{1 - p_i*} \tag{2.28}$$

where $p_i*$ is the element of the $i$th row, $i$th column of $\mathbf{R}*$. Let us finally call the Prais index $w_i*$. We have

$$w_i* = \frac{1/(1 - r_{ii})}{1/(1 - p_i*)} = \frac{1 - p_i*}{1 - r_{ii}} \tag{2.29}$$

or, substituting eqn. (2.25) into eqn. (2.29)

$$w_i* = \frac{1 - p_i*}{1 - p_{ii}/p_{(0)i}} = \frac{p_{(0)i}(1 - p_i*)}{p_{(0)i} - p_{ii}} \tag{2.30}$$

Let us finally call $j$ those who are not $i$. Then

$$w_i* = \frac{p_{(0)i} p_j*}{p_{ij}} \tag{2.31}$$

Then, by eqns. (2.27) and (2.31), the relationship between the Prais index and the reformulated index is very simple, namely

$$w_i*/w_i** = p_j*/p_{(1)j} \tag{2.32}$$

TABLE 2.1

The Prais' index and its non-equilibrium version applied to Glass' data

| Social group | Actual distri-bution of sons | Equilibrium distribution | $w_i*$ | $w_i**$ | $w_i*$ corrected |
|---|---|---|---|---|---|
| Professional | 0.029 | 0.023 | 0.79 | 0.78 | 1.79 |
| Managerial | 0.046 | 0.042 | 0.91 | 0.91 | 1.33 |
| Higher grade non manual | 0.094 | 0.088 | 0.94 | 0.93 | 1.13 |
| Lower grade non manual | 0.131 | 0.127 | 0.97 | 0.96 | 1.13 |
| Skilled manual | 0.409 | 0.409 | 1.00 | 1.00 | 1.14 |
| Semi-skilled manual | 0.170 | 0.182 | 1.07 | 1.08 | 1.22 |
| Unskilled manual | 0.121 | 0.129 | 1.07 | 1.08 | 1.21 |

We reproduce, in Table 2.1, the results drawn by Prais from Glass' mobility study. In the fourth column, we have computed, using eqn. (2.32), the values of the index $w_i**$. As expected, they are not very different from the values of $w_i*$.

*Correction for changes in the occupational structure*

Let us add that Prais was, of course, aware that changes in the occupational structure were not actually taken into account by his index. He proposed to correct this defect in the following way. Let us consider the marginals of $\mathbf{P}$, the observed turnover matrix, and build from these marginals a minimum mobility turnover matrix, using the assumption that a growing category draws its growth from the nearest declining category. Let us then transform this turnover matrix into a transition matrix by dividing its elements by the appropriate row total and call the result $\mathbf{R}(1)$. Then, this is the transition matrix we should observe if shifts in the occupational structure are the only source of mobility.

We suppose, then, that the distribution of individuals from one generation to the next is a two-stage process. In the first stage, families move as a consequence of shifts in the occupational structure. These moves are described by $\mathbf{R}(1)$. Then they are moved again according to say $\mathbf{R}(2)$, so that

$$\mathbf{R} = \mathbf{R}(1)\,\mathbf{R}(2) \tag{2.33}$$

The matrix $R(2)$ may be considered as describing the moves not accounted for by shifts in the occupational structure. By eqn. (2.33)

$$\mathbf{R}(2) = \mathbf{R}(1)^{-1}\mathbf{R} \tag{2.34}$$

The derivation leading either to $w_i*$ or to $w_i**$ may then be applied to $\mathbf{R}(2)$ rather than to $\mathbf{R}$. This leads to two new indices, say, $z_i*$ and $z_i**$. The latter is simply, by eqn. (2.27), the reciprocal of the Glass index applied to $\mathbf{D}_0\mathbf{R}(2)$. The former is somewhat more complicated, since it uses the equilibrium distribution, but it is structurally closely related to the latter. Thus, while the $z$ indices are certainly preferable to the $w$ indices, since the former take into account shifts in the occupational structure and the others do not, it is difficult to say which of $z_i*$ and $z_i**$ should be preferred. Perhaps, the introduction of the equilibrium distribution is a useless complication since, at any rate, this distribution can only be used as a characterization of the current situation and not for prediction.

50

## 2.3. Another application of Markov chain theory to social mobility measurement: Bartholomew's index

We shall now turn to an interesting index originally proposed by Bartholomew (1967). This index assumes that the social categories are ordered. Note that this assumption is very frequently, but not systematically, made in social mobility measurement: the index $I_B$ of the previous chapter or the index $z_i^*$ introduce this assumption; but Prais' original index $w_i^{**}$ as well as the Matras index, $M_M$, for instance, do not.

The main innovation of Bartholomew's index is that it takes account, not only of the number of moves as does, for instance, the Matras index $M_M$ or $M_S$ (Section 1.5), but also of the distance covered by a mover. This distance is measured by the number of boundaries between social categories crossed by a family from one generation to the next. As previously, let $p_{(0)i}$ be the proportion of fathers belonging to social category $i$ and $r_{ij}$ describe the transition rate from category $i$ to category $j$. Then

$$M_C = N \sum_{i=1}^{\sigma} \sum_{j=1}^{\sigma} p_{(0)i} r_{ij} |i-j|$$

$$= N \sum_{i=1}^{\sigma} \sum_{j=1}^{\sigma} p_{ij} |i-j|$$

$$= \sum_{i=1}^{\sigma} \sum_{j=1}^{\sigma} n_{ij} |i-j| \tag{2.35}$$

gives the number of class boundaries crossed from one generation to the next.

This is, of course, a counting index, although of a more refined type than $M_M$, the Matras index. Dividing eqn. (2.35) by $N$ gives the average number of boundaries crossed by a family and thus makes the index independent of the size of the population. However, the index cannot easily be used in the form originally presented by Bartholomew, since it does not take into account the effect of the shifts in the occupational structure.

One way of eliminating this effect is, for instance, to refer $M_C$ to the minimum possible value this index can have when the only source of mobility arises from the shifts in the occupational structure. Let us call this quantity $M_{C\,min}$. It gives the number of boundaries crossed by $N$ families when the mobility is purely structural, *i.e.* minimum.

In order to obtain $M_{C\min}$, we have first to locate as many families as possible on the diagonal of $\mathbf{P}$, the turnover matrix*. If we do so, we have in row $i$ a number $m_{(0)i}^0$ of families crossing no boundaries with

$$m_{(0)i}^0 = \min(n_{(0)i}, n_{(1)i}) \tag{2.36}$$

and $m_{(1)j}^0$ families in column $j$ crossing no boundaries with

$$m_{(1)j}^0 = \min(n_{(0)j}, n_{(1)j}) \tag{2.37}$$

Then, there remain, after this first step

$$n_{(0)i}^1 = n_{(0)i} - m_{(0)i}^0 \tag{2.38}$$

movers in row $i$ and

$$n_{(1)j}^1 = n_{(1)j} - m_{(1)j}^0 \tag{2.39}$$

movers in column $j$. Let us now call $m_{(0)i}^1$ the maximum number of one-boundary movers in row $i$ under the assumption of minimum mobility. It is readily verified that

$$m_{(0)i}^1 = \min(n_{(0)i}^1, n_{(1)(i-1)}^1 + n_{(1)(i+1)}^1) \tag{2.40}$$

where $n_{(1)(i-1)}^1$ and $n_{(1)(i+1)}^1$ are assumed equal to zero if $(i-1)$ is smaller than 1 or $(i+1)$ greater than $\sigma$. In the same way, the maximum number of one-boundary movers in column $j$ is

$$m_{(1)j}^1 = \min(n_{(1)j}^1, n_{(0)(j-1)}^1 + n_{(0)(j+1)}^1) \tag{2.41}$$

If we remove these one-boundary movers, we obtain in row $i$

---

* As pointed out to me by David McFarland, the concept of minimum mobility as defined here is not completely unambiguous. Thus, let us assume $\mathbf{n}_0 = (200, 100, 100, 100)$ and $\mathbf{n}_1 = (100, 100, 100, 200)$. The procedure used here will generate a minimum mobility matrix characterized by 400 units located in the main diagonal and 100 crossing three boundaries. But we could also introduce an alternative definition of minimum mobility such that 200 units would be located in the main diagonal while 300 would cross one boundary.

$$n_{(0)i}{}^2 = n_{(0)i}{}^1 - m_{(0)i}{}^1 \tag{2.42}$$

families that cross at least two-boundaries. In the same way,

$$n_{(1)j}{}^2 = n_{(1)j}{}^1 - m_{(1)j}{}^1 \tag{2.43}$$

families cross at least two-boundaries in column $j$.

Continuing in the same way, we see that the maximum number of families crossing only two boundaries is

$$m_{(0)i}{}^2 = \min(n_{(0)i}{}^2, \, n_{(1)(i-2)}{}^2 + n_{(1)(i+2)}{}^2) \tag{2.44}$$

in row $i$ and

$$m_{(1)j}{}^2 = \min(n_{(1)j}{}^2, \, n_{(0)(j-2)}{}^2 + n_{(0)(j+2)}{}^2) \tag{2.45}$$

in column $j$. Following the same procedure up to $(\sigma - 1)$, since $(\sigma - 1)$ boundaries at most can be crossed, we obtain the maximum number of boundaries crossed under the assumption of minimum mobility

$$M_{C\min} = \sum_{i=1}^{\sigma} \sum_{k=1}^{\sigma-1} k m_{(0)i}{}^k$$

$$= \sum_{i=1}^{\sigma} \sum_{k=1}^{\sigma-1} k \min(n_{(0)i}{}^k, \, n_{(1)(i-k)}{}^k + n_{(1)(i+k)}{}^k) \tag{2.46}$$

or, alternatively, using columns rather than rows

$$M_{C\min} = \sum_{j=1}^{\sigma} \sum_{k=1}^{\sigma-1} k m_{(1)j}{}^k$$

$$= \sum_{j=1}^{\sigma} \sum_{k=1}^{\sigma-1} k \min(n_{(1)j}{}^k, \, n_{(0)(j-k)}{}^k + n_{(0)(j+k)}{}^k) \tag{2.47}$$

Finally, we define a mobility index by referring $M_C$ to $M_{C\min}$. Let us call this index $b$. It can, for instance, take the following form.

$$b = (M_C - M_{C\min})/M_{C\min} \tag{2.48}$$

It is 0 when the actual amount of mobility is equal to the amount of mobility generated by the shifts in the occupational distribution and increases with an increase in the amount of non-structural or exchange mobility.

A better index could, of course, be devised: it would measure $M_C$, the actual amount of mobility in Bartholomew's sense, taking as a unit the difference between $M_{Cmax}$, the number of boundaries which would be crossed if mobility were maximum and $M_{Cmin}$. This index would have the advantage of having definite upper and lower boundaries, whereas the upper boundary of $b$ is ill-defined. We shall not develop this index here since $M_{Cmax}$, as $M_{Cmin}$, can in practice be very easily determined, while the mathematical formula is complicated and space-consuming. In the dichotomous case, this index is the same as $M_B$ (Chapter 1, Section 1.4) and the reformulated Matras index $M_S$ (Chapter 1, Section 1.5).

Let us add that we chose to introduce Bartholomew's index and its variations in this chapter, rather than in Chapter 1, because Bartholomew suggests substituting, in eqn. (2.35), $p_i^*$, the proportion of people in class $i$ in the equilibrium distribution, for $p_{(0)i}$, the proportion of fathers in class $i$. This suggestion parallels that of Prais (Section 2.2). However, taking the equilibrium class structure and the equilibrium transition matrix rather than the class structure at the fathers' generation and the observed transition matrix, has the effect that

$$M_{Cmin} = 0 \tag{2.49}$$

This results from the fact that, at equilibrium,

$$\mathbf{p}^* = \mathbf{p}^*\mathbf{R} \tag{2.50}$$

so that the amount of structural mobility is necessarily 0. In fact, Bartholomew proposes to substitute the equilibrium class structure for the class structure of the fathers' generation, without substituting the equilibrium matrix for the observed transition matrix.

## 2.4. A derived measure of inheritance; first application of the mover—stayer distinction

We shall now turn to an important research tradition which has both a general relevance to the mathematical theory of social mobility and also a special interest for mobility measurement. This tradition originated with the pioneering work of Blumen et al. (1955, 1966) on the mover—stayer model. As we shall see below, this model gives rise to many variations, some of which are of the utmost interest for the mathematical theory of social mobility.

*The original mover—stayer model*

Blumen's original model deals with labor turnover, *i.e.* with intragenerational mobility. The model is derived basically from the empirical finding that job mobility appears always to be weaker than would be expected under the assumption of a Markov chain. Assume, in other words, that an observed transition matrix $\mathbf{R}$ describes the ways the workers of a population move from one occupational category to another from the beginning to the end of, say, a quarter. Then we may try to predict the turnover after $t$ quarters using the assumption that the process follows the axioms of a Markov chain. In this case $\mathbf{R}^t$, *i.e.* $\mathbf{R}$ raised to the $t$th power, predicts the turnover between the initial quarter, 0, and quarter $t$, while

$$\mathbf{p}_0 \mathbf{R}^t = \mathbf{p}_t \tag{2.51}$$

predicts the occupational structure at the $t$th quarter. However, the diagonal elements of $\mathbf{R}^t$ will generally be much smaller than the diagonal elements of the empirical matrix, say $\mathbf{R}^{(t)}$, which gives the observed transition rates between quarter 0 and quarter $t$.

In order to account for this general empirical observation, Blumen and his colleagues proposed to consider the population as composed of two latent categories of people: the stayers and the movers. The movers are supposed to move according to a Markov chain. The stayers simply stay. In other words, they are supposed to stay with a probability equal to 1. Let us, for instance, consider $r_{ii}$, the proportion of people located in occupational category $i$ at the beginning of quarter 0 who are still in category $i$ at the beginning of quarter 1. This proportion will be considered as the sum of two latent components: $s_i$, the proportion of the stayers in category $i$, and $(1-s_i)m_{ii}$ where the proportion of movers is $(1-s_i)$ and these movers have a probability $m_{ii}$ of moving from $i$ to $i$, *i.e.* of staying, though they are movers. Then,

$$r_{ii} = s_i + (1 - s_i)m_{ii} \tag{2.52}$$

55

or, in matrix form,

$$\mathbf{R} = \mathbf{S} + (\mathbf{I} - \mathbf{S})\mathbf{M} \tag{2.53}$$

where $\mathbf{R} = [r_{ij}]$ is the observed transition matrix, $\mathbf{S}$ the diagonal matrix $\text{diag}[s_i]$, $\mathbf{I}$ the identity matrix and $\mathbf{M} = [m_{ij}]$ the transition matrix of movers.

### White's intergenerational mover—stayer model

We shall return later to the original mover—stayer model. For the moment, we shall deal with some adaptations of this model to intergenerational mobility. Obviously, this adaptation is possible: we may, in the intergenerational case as in the intragenerational, introduce the latent distinction between stayers and movers. If this distinction leads to consistent models, it may be used to solve the problem of measuring social mobility. Nonetheless, there is an important difference between intergenerational and intragenerational mobility, *i.e.* the size of the time unit. As a consequence, in the intragenerational case it may be possible, as in Blumen's example, to observe a sequence of mobility matrices. In the intergenerational case, a single, or at most a very small number, of matrices will be available. Thus, model (2.53) clearly cannot be directly applied to intergenerational mobility. With a single matrix, the equations of this model cannot be solved. The models to be presented below are derived from the original mover—stayer model in the sense that, as with this latter model, they introduce a distinction between two latent sub-populations. However, their mathematical structure is distinct from that of the original model.

One of the most interesting applications of the mover—stayer idea to intergenerational mobility is provided by White (1970b). In fact, White proposes two models more or less directly inspired by the mover—stayer distinction (1963, 1970b). In this section, we shall analyze the most recent of these contributions.

The "modified inheritance model", as White calls it, assumes, as does Blumen's model, that each social category $i$ includes an unknown proportion of movers. Let us call $s_i$ the number of stayers in $i$ and $m_{ii}$ the number of movers who happen to stay in $i$. (Note that to avoid the proliferation of symbols, these symbols have a slightly different meaning here from that in the previous subsection.) Otherwise, let us use our traditional notation. Then, $n_{ij}$ is the number of sons with father $i$ who are themselves $j$; $n_{(0)i}$ the number of fathers in stratum $i$; $n_{(1)j}$ the number of sons in stratum $j$, etc. On the other hand, let us call $m_{ij}$ the number of movers going from $i$ to $j$, $m_{(0)i}$ the number of movers whose father belongs to category $i$ and $m_{(1)j}$ the number of movers among the sons currently belonging to social category $j$.

The first equation of the model is

$$n_{ii} = m_{ii} + (n_{(0)i} - m_{(0)i}) \qquad (2.54)$$

This equation states that the total observed number of families staying in $i$ from one generation to the next is the sum of the number of movers who stay in $i$ and of the number of stayers. Note that in the intergenerational case, the attributes "mover" and "stayer" apply to families and not to individuals.

A second equation states that all the families who move from $i$ to $j$ belong to the class of movers

$$n_{ij} = m_{ij} \qquad (2.55)$$

Of course, the equations cannot be solved without further assumptions. In the case of Blumen's original model, the estimation of $S$, the diagonal matrix describing the proportions of stayers, was possible because of the assumption that $M$ generates a Markov chain. As we shall see below, Blumen and his colleagues used $M^*$, the equilibrium matrix, for this estimation. Here, since we have only one matrix, a functional substitute, so to speak, must be found. White derives this substitute by using the traditional assumption of perfect mobility. This assumption is, of course, only applied to the movers. Then

$$m_{ij} = \frac{m_{(0)i} \cdot m_{(1)j}}{M} \qquad (2.56)$$

where $M$ gives the total number of movers.

By eqns. (2.54) and (2.55), the difference between $n_{(0)i}$ and $n_{(1)i}$ is equal to the difference between the number of movers who really moved in the $i$th row and the number of movers who really moved in the $i$th column.

$$n_{(0)1} - n_{(1)i} = (m_{(0)i} - m_{ii}) - (m_{(1)i} - m_{ii})$$

$$= m_{(0)i} - m_{(1)i} \qquad (2.57)$$

Hence,

$$m_{(1)i} = m_{(0)i} - (n_{(0)i} - n_{(1)i}) \qquad (2.58)$$

Substituting eqns. (2.56) and (2.58) into eqn. (2.54), we obtain

$$n_{ii} = \frac{m_{(0)i}(m_{(0)i} - n_{(0)i} + n_{(1)i})}{M} + (n_{(0)i} - m_{(0)i}) \qquad (2.59)$$

which defines a set of quadratic equations connected by their sum. In order to solve them, White proposes to choose an initial value for $M$, say $M_0$, to check that $M_0$ leads to real roots, to solve for $m_{(0)i}$, to take $\Sigma m_{(0)i}$ as a new trial value and to repeat the operation until the trial value for $M$ equals $\Sigma m_{(0)i}$.

Since the inequality

$$(M + n_{(0)i} - n_{(1)i})^2 - 4(n_{(0)i} - n_{ii}) M \geqslant 0 \qquad (2.60)$$

must hold in order for the roots to be real, a reasonably large initial value for $M_0$ is generally advisable. In most applications, $n_{(0)i} - n_{(1)i}$ is indeed rather small. If this difference is zero, then $M$ should be chosen to be greater than $4(n_{(0)i} - n_{ii})$.

We will not examine in more detail the problem of solving eqn. (2.59). This is a technical problem and we prefer to refer the reader to White's original text. The logical and substantive interest of the model proposed by White is more important for our purpose*.

In one of the applications presented, White used his model for analyzing British and Danish trichotomous mobility tables. He found that the model applied in neither of the two cases: it was impossible to fit acceptable values for $m_{(0)1}$, $m_{(0)2}$ and $m_{(0)3}$ simultaneously. This negative result shows that the data to which the model was applied are incompatible with the assumptions described by eqns. (2.54)—(2.56) according to which the population could be divided into two latent sub-populations, i.e. a sub-population of stayers and one of movers submitted to the rule of perfect mobility.

White then proceeded with further assumptions. He found a good fit for $m_{(0)1}$ and $m_{(0)3}$ when the supplementary assumption

$$m_{(0)2} = n_{(0)2} \qquad (2.61)$$

---

* A maximum likelihood solution of White's model is presented in the statistical appendix.

is introduced, *i.e.* when everybody is supposed to be a mover in social category 2. In another application, White used Blau and Duncan's data and obtained a good fit. He then computed what he calls the "inheritance fraction". Let us call this index $I_W$, defined by

$$I_{W(i)} = 1 - (m_{(0)i}/n_{(0)i}) \tag{2.62}$$

The inheritance fraction is, in other words, the proportion of stayers in a given social category. In applying this index to Blau and Duncan's data, White found the rather small average value of 0.092. The index reaches a moderately large value only for the professionals (professional, self-employed: 0.156; professional, salaried: 0.240) and for the farmers (0.153). However, the fit of the off-diagonal elements of the mobility matrix is, according to the author, rather poor.

Needless to say, the inheritance fraction is a very interesting measure of immobility. When the fit is good for the diagonal elements of a mobility matrix, it provides a very useful description of the structure of this matrix.

It must be noted that a poor fit for the off-diagonal elements of a matrix does not imply that the model should be rejected. Indeed, it is possible to split eqn. (2.56) into two sub-sets of equations.

$$m_{ij} = \frac{m_{(0)i} \cdot m_{(1)j}}{M} \qquad (i = j) \tag{2.63a}$$

$$m_{ij} = \frac{m_{(0)i} \cdot m_{(1)j}}{M} \qquad (i \neq j) \tag{2.63b}$$

Now, eqn. (2.59) which permits determination of the $m_{(0)i}$ values, *i.e.* the numbers of movers in each row, is derived from eqns. (2.54), (2.58) and (2.63a). On the other hand, obviously eqn. (2.63a) may hold and eqn. (2.63b) not hold. Thus, White's model is actually composed of two distinct versions. The first version is defined by eqns. (2.54), (2.55) and (2.63a) and states that the movers move according to the rule of perfect mobility exclusively when they happen to go from $i$ to $i$, *i.e.* when they happen to stay. Otherwise, perfect mobility is not assumed. The only criterion for rejecting or accepting the model is, in this case, the quality of the fit with respect to the diagonal elements of the mobility matrix.

A restricted version of the model is obtained when assumption

(2.63b) is added to the assumptions (2.54), (2.55) and (2.63a) of the previous version. It is restricted in the sense that a supplementary assumption is introduced. Here, the test of the model is that it provides a good fit for all elements, diagonal and off-diagonal, of the mobility matrix.

In other words, in the first (general) version of the model, nothing is specified about $m_{ij}$ ($i \neq j$) except that $m_{ij}$ is the number of true movers going from $i$ to $j$. Thus, with a good fit for the diagonal elements of the mobility matrix, the inheritance fraction may be computed, giving genuine information about the differential structure of immobility according to social category.

### A simplified version of White's model: Goodman's model

Goodman (1965) has proposed, in one of his papers, a model which may be considered as a particular version of White's model. It should be noted that Goodman's model predates White's model.

In White's model, while the stayers have a zero probability of moving, the movers have a non-zero probability of staying, as shown by eqn. (2.63a). In Goodman's model, the assumptions for the two latent sub-populations are symmetric: the stayers are not allowed to move and the movers are not allowed to stay.

With this assumption, eqn. (2.54) reduces to

$$n_{ii} = n_{(0)i} - m_{(0)i} \tag{2.64}$$

since

$$m_{ii} = 0 \tag{2.65}$$

The other assumptions of White's model, eqns. (2.55) and (2.56), are retained: the movers are, in other words, supposed to move according to the rule of perfect mobility. In summary, Goodman's model may be derived from the strong (restricted) version of White's model by substituting eqn. (2.65) for eqn. (2.63a).

This substitution makes Goodman's model, by contrast with White's, very simple. While in White's model the estimation of the number of stayers in each category is complicated, it becomes very simple in Goodman's model, since the stayers are those who are located in the main diagonal of a mobility matrix. Thus, the procedure for testing the adequateness of the model is very simple.

The first step consists in subtracting the diagonal figures from the corresponding row and column marginals and in blanking out these diagonal figures. This gives the numbers $m_{(0)i}$ of movers in each row and the numbers $m_{(1)j}$ of movers in each column.

The next and final step is to verify that

$$m_{ij} = \frac{m_{(0)i} \cdot m_{(1)j}}{M} \qquad (i \neq j) \qquad\qquad (2.66)$$

where, as in the White's model,

$$m_{ij} = n_{ij} \qquad\qquad (i \neq j) \qquad\qquad (2.67)$$

Goodman has proposed several variations of this simple model. Let us suppose, for instance, a trichotomous mobility table. In the version of the model which has just been described, the families located in the main diagonal are all considered as stayers: an inheritance phenomenon is assumed in each social category and the degree of this inheritance is simply measured by the proportion of families belonging to the $i$th row that are located in the $i$th column.

An alternative assumption supposes that an inheritance phenomenon is at work in some social categories, say categories 1 and 3, but not in the other, category 2. Then, $n_{11}$ and $n_{33}$ are, as previously, considered to describe the numbers of stayers respectively in categories 1 and 3. The quantity $n_{22}$ is considered to describe a sub-population of, so to speak, apparent stayers, $i.e.$ of families that are movers but happen to stay. With this assumption, the test of the model includes the following steps.

(1) Subtract the diagonal figures from the corresponding row and column totals for the categories in which a social inheritance is assumed, $i.e.$ in our example, categories 1 and 3, and blank out these diagonal cells.

(2) Keep the original row and column totals for the social categories where no social inheritance is assumed (in our example, for category 2).

(3) Verify that

$$m_{ij} = \frac{m_{(0)i} \cdot m_{(1)j}}{M} \qquad\qquad (2.68)$$

(for all cells not blanked out).

Thus, in our example, where social inheritance applies only to categories 1 and 3, we have to verify that eqn. (2.68) holds for all cells except the blanked out diagonal cells corresponding to these categories.

Similar variations can also be introduced in White's model: we may also suppose in this model that some diagonal cells contain no stayers.

Of course, any other similar variation is possible: for each social category, we may choose either to assume or not to assume the action of social inheritance. In presenting applications of his model, Goodman has shown that the best fit is generally obtained by assuming a social inheritance effect in all social categories.

Goodman's model has a great advantage in its simplicity. On the other hand, this advantage is the consequence of the rigidity of the assumptions. Either we assume the action of a social inheritance effect in a given social category, say $i$, and the families of row $i$ located in column $i$ are *all* considered as *stayers*. Or we do not assume this action and the same families are *all* considered as *movers*, even if they happen to stay. Even with a good fit, it is hard to accept, from a sociological point of view, that the effect of social inheritance could be zero in some social categories. White's assumption that the families located in the diagonal cells are of two kinds, a latent sub-population of movers and a latent sub-population of stayers, is undoubtedly more appealing for a sociologist, even if it leads to greater mathematical complications.

*Three types of mover—stayer models applied to intergenerational mobility*

Goodman's model is characterized by the assumption that the stayers are not allowed to move and the movers not allowed to stay. More exactly, the stayers are never allowed to move and the movers are only allowed to stay when there are no stayers already in a given social category.

By contrast, White's model assumes that the movers are always allowed to stay. In other words, the diagonal cells of a mobility matrix can include stayers *and* movers, while in Goodman's model they include stayers *or* movers, but not both. On the other hand White's model makes the same assumption as Goodman's for the stayers: they are never allowed to move.

Let us ignore, for a moment, the variations that Goodman has proposed for his model and consider its basic version described by the eqns. (2.64)—(2.66). Then, we can summarize the fundamental difference between White's and Goodman's models as in Table 2.2.

TABLE 2.2

Three types of mover—stayer models with their assumptions

| | |
|---|---|
| Type 1 model (Goodman's model) | Movers not allowed to stay, stayers not allowed to move |
| Type 2 model (White's model) | Movers allowed to stay, stayers not allowed to move |
| Type 3 model | Movers (LC1 people) allowed to stay, stayers (LC2 people) allowed to move |

Here, we have called Goodman's model a Type 1 model: the families in the diagonal are all stayers. White's model is called a Type 2 model. Here the families on the diagonal are partially movers and partially stayers, while the off-diagonal cells contain only movers.

This presentation suggests a third type of model given at the bottom of the table. In this model, which was proposed by the author (1973a), the stayers are allowed to move, exactly as the movers are allowed to stay in White's model. We call this a Type 3 model and develop it in the next section.

A general point is worth mentioning concerning this Type 3 model. While Table 2.2 shows that this model appears, at the mathematical level, as a natural extension of the Type 1 and Type 2 models, it does raise a semantic problem. Indeed, in Goodman's or in White's model it is very easy to follow the stayers, since, by the assumptions of these models, they are always located on the diagonal. With the Type 3 model, the symmetry of the assumptions with regard to the latent sub-populations has the consequence that the semantic interpretation of these sub-populations as stayers and movers becomes impossible. Thus, the model we shall present belongs on the one hand to the mover—stayer family of models; but it has, on the other hand, a different interpretation and other uses.

## 2.5. A general model for the analysis of mobility tables: the Type 3 model

In the exposition of this model, we shall substitute a distinction between latent class 1 people (LC1) and latent class 2 (LC2) people for the distinction between movers and stayers. Provisionally, we shall retain the symbols $m$ and $s$ to describe the two classes. This distinction will be interpreted and generalized later.

63

## The two latent class version of the Type 3 model

We shall suppose, as previously, that $n_{ij}$ is the observed number of families in cell $(i, j)$ of the mobility matrix. For all $i$ and all $j$, $n_{ij}$ will be the sum of $m_{ij}$, the number of LC1 people, and $s_{ij}$, the number of LC2 people located in the cell $(i, j)$.

$$n_{ij} = m_{ij} + s_{ij} \qquad (2.69)$$

It is readily verified that, if we suppose $s_{ij} = 0$ for $i \neq j$, we return to White's eqns. (2.54) and (2.55).

The second equation of the model is the same as eqn. (2.56) of White's model.

$$m_{ij} = \frac{m_{(0)i} \cdot m_{(1)j}}{M} \qquad (2.70)$$

This equation states that the LC1 people move according to the rule of perfect mobility. $M$ is the total number of LC1 people.

An equivalent assumption will be made for the LC2 people

$$s_{ij} = \frac{s_{(0)i} \cdot s_{(1)j}}{S} \qquad (2.71)$$

where $S$ is the total number of LC2 people. Thus, $s_{ij}$, the number of LC2 people moving from $i$ to $j$, is the product of the number of LC1 people who come from $i$ and the proportion of those who go to $j$. In other words, within the latent class 2, the destination of the moves is supposed to be independent of their origin. The same is true for the latent class 1.

Equations (2.70) and (2.71) reveal why it is impossible to keep the semantic distinction (movers—stayers) used in Goodman's and

TABLE 2.3

A fictitious intergenerational mobility matrix

| Fathers' social category | Sons' social category | | | | |
|---|---|---|---|---|---|
| | 1 | 2 | 3 | 4 | Total |
| 1 | 1090 | 550 | 170 | 190 | 2000 |
| 2 | 2170 | 1090 | 260 | 280 | 3800 |
| 3 | 260 | 170 | 655 | 815 | 1900 |
| 4 | 280 | 190 | 815 | 1015 | 2300 |
| Total | 3800 | 2000 | 1900 | 2300 | 10000 |

in White's model. In the Type 3 model, the two sub-populations must behave symmetrically and thus are interchangeable.

Let us, as an illustration, consider the fictitious matrix reproduced in Table 2.3. Applying the Type 3 model to this matrix, we find the following values for the parameters*.

$m_{(0)1} = 1800$   $m_{(0)2} = 3600$   $m_{(0)3} = 300$   $m_{(0)4} = 300$

$m_{(1)1} = 3600$   $m_{(1)2} = 1800$   $m_{(1)3} = 300$   $m_{(1)4} = 300$

$s_{(0)1} = 200$   $s_{(0)2} = 200$   $s_{(0)3} = 1600$   $s_{(0)4} = 2000$

$s_{(1)1} = 200$   $s_{(1)2} = 200$   $s_{(1)3} = 1600$   $s_{(1)4} = 2000$

$M = 6000$   $S = 4000$

The interpretation of this solution is that behind the four manifest social categories, we have two latent classes. The first one is characterized by the fact that its members are likely to come from social categories 1 and 2 or to go to categories 1 and 2. They are much less likely to come from categories 3 and 4 or to go to these categories. Reciprocally, the LC2 people circulate between social categories 3 and 4, with few of them coming from or going to social categories 1 and 2.

This example illustrates the kind of uses the Type 3 model may have. It also shows that the semantic distinction between stayers and movers has to be dropped.

While this model is an extension of White's model, the introduction of the possibility of any of the sub-populations moving or staying changes the interpretation of these sub-populations. In Goodman's model, the observed mobility matrix is split into a sum of two components. The first component is a diagonal matrix, the elements of which are either the corresponding elements of the observed mobility matrix or zero (for the categories where no inheritance effect is postulated). The second component is the difference matrix between the observed matrix and this diagonal matrix.

---

* In fact the computations were made the other way round: the fictitious intergenerational mobility matrix of Table 2.3 was generated with the help of the following parameters. For the solution of the model, see the statistical appendix.

In White's model, the observed matrix is again split into two components: the diagonal matrix of stayers and the difference matrix corresponding to the movers.

Here, in the Type 3 model, the observed matrix is again a sum of two components, both being non-diagonal matrices following the same rule as the second component of Goodman's or of White's model, *i.e.* perfect mobility. Thus, finally, the rationale for this model is to decompose the circulation system described by a mobility matrix into a sum of sub-systems characterized by freedom of circulation, in the sense that, according to the concept of perfect mobility, the arrival category is independent of the departure category. Of course, the sum of two perfect mobility matrices will not generally be a perfect mobility matrix.

*Extension of the Type 3 model to g latent classes*

Since the semantic distinction stayers/movers has to be abandoned, nothing prevents us from supposing that an observed non-perfect mobility matrix may be decomposable into more than 2 perfect mobility components. We may, for instance, wish to reproduce an observed matrix as the sum of 3 perfect mobility matrices. In this case, we speak of a three-class model*.

Of course, the number of latent classes which may be introduced is dependent on the number of social categories which appear in the observed mobility matrix. Let us suppose, for instance, that the number of latent classes, 2 in the previous description of the model, is now $g$. This situation will introduce $(2\sigma-1)$ independent parameters for each class except one or, for $g$ classes, $(2\sigma-1) \times (g-1)$ independent parameters, giving the numbers of families going to and coming from the social categories in each latent class.

The number of independent empirical quantities is equal to $(\sigma-1)^2$. Thus, for the model to be determinate, $g$ must be chosen small enough, so that the inequality

$$(2\sigma-1)(g-1) \leqslant (\sigma-1)^2 \Rightarrow g \leqslant \frac{\sigma^2}{2\sigma-1} \qquad (2.72)$$

holds. With $\sigma = 4$ or 5, $g$ cannot be greater than 2. With $\sigma = 6$, $g$ cannot be greater than 3, etc. This means that if a mobility matrix

---

* The reader might wish to compare this generalized version of the intergenerational movers—stayers model with the latent structure models. See, for instance, Lazarsfeld and Henry (1968).

with 6 social categories cannot be decomposed into a sum of $g = 2$ latent perfect mobility matrices, we may try $g = 3$.

The problem raised by the solution of the Type 3 model will not be dealt with here. As the inequality (2.72) shows, the number of parameters will generally be smaller than the number of degrees of freedom of the observed matrix. Thus, generally, there will be no unique algebraic solution of the model. A maximum likelihood solution of the model for the general case of $g$ latent classes is presented in the statistical appendix.

## 2.6. Structural methods, an overview

The models analyzed in the previous sections are clearly not only interesting for being, in most cases, measurement models. They also provide, in general, a rationale for what may be called a structural analysis of the intergenerational mobility matrices. The last model is interesting in this respect. Although directly derived from Goodman's and from White's versions of the mover—stayer model, it leads less to mobility measures than to a structural analysis of the mobility matrices. Sometimes, the distinction between measurement and structural analysis may even be difficult. Thus, the Prais model exposed in Section 2.2 leads, rather than to a single index, to a set of indices giving the average waiting time to which a family belonging to a given social category is exposed before being able to change position. This set of indices may be considered as providing a structural analysis of a mobility matrix. Bartholomew's index, or rather the standardized version of this index which is proposed in Section 2.3, was presented as an overall index. Returning to eqns. (2.35) et seq., we see, however, that it would be possible, by restricting the summation to the rows to define a set of indices which would describe the number of boundaries crossed by a family having given social origin, beyond the number of boundary-crossings imposed by the marginals. The result could again be called a structural analysis of a mobility table.

All three versions of the mover—stayer model studied in Sections 2.4 and 2.5 are also structural methods as well as being measurement models. This is clear, as we saw in the case of the last model. But it is also true for Goodman's and White's models. In Goodman's model, the proportion of stayers is an overall mobility index. But this is only a by-product of the model. Its main interest lies in telling us whether a given mobility table may be reproduced using the assumption that some social categories, at least, may be considered as composed of two distinct sub-populations: the stayers that inherit, so to speak, their social status, and the movers whose achievement is independent of their original status.

White's model is not only a measurement model, but also a method of structural analysis applicable to mobility tables, since this model may be considered as an effort to refine Goodman's model. The application of the model will, here again, provide a picture of the differential inheritance structure underlying a mobility matrix.

There are, of course, many other structural models or methods that may be applied to the analysis of mobility tables. To present them exhaustively would, however, be beyond the scope and intentions of this book. Thus, we shall be content briefly to evoke several other models.

Let us first turn to a model which is worth mentioning because of its close relationship both to Goodman's and to White's models as analyzed in the previous sections. This model is also due to White (1963). As in the case of Goodman's model, the first step is to blank out some cells of the mobility matrix to be analyzed. These blanked out cells will generally be diagonal: they include the families that, by hypothesis, are considered as excluded from the perfect mobility allocation process which rules the moves of the remaining families. As we see, the model is very close to Goodman's.

The next step is to consider the probability that exactly $n_{ij}$ individuals appear in cell $(i,j)$, given the marginals of the mobility matrix. The resulting formula is

$$p(n_{ij}) = \frac{\prod\limits_{i=1}^{\sigma} (n_{(0)i}!) \prod\limits_{j=1}^{\sigma} (n_{(1)j}!)}{(n!)\left[ \prod\limits_{i=1}^{\sigma} \prod\limits_{j=1}^{\sigma} n_{ij} \right]} \tag{2.73}$$

The basic idea of this model inspired Goodman's model. The only difference concerns the statistical tests which are to be used to evaluate the fit between the model and a set of data. White's model supposes the marginals to be fixed, while Goodman's model does not.

Goodman (1969a) has proposed an interesting descriptive method for the analysis of mobility tables which is also worth mentioning. The general approach of this method is the following.

(1) Consider at each step of the analysis only 2 of the origin categories and 2 of the destination categories.

(2) Characterize each of the resulting dichotomies by what Goodman calls the "odds-ratios" (see below).

(3) Compare these odds-ratios.

Let us, for instance, consider a trichotomous table. A first dichotomy will include origin (input) categories 1 and 2 and destination (output) categories 1 and 2. Now, $n_{11}/n_{12}$ is the odds for families coming from 1 going to 1 rather than to 2, while $n_{21}/n_{22}$ is the odds for families from 2 going, similarly, to 1 rather than to 2. The ratio of these odds will be the odds-ratio characteristic of the input categories 1 and 2 and of the output categories 1 and 2. In the same way, it is possible to define an odds-ratio, say for input categories 1 and 3 and for output categories 2 and 3. As there are three pairs of input categories and of output categories in a trichotomous table, the table will be characterized by nine odds-ratios. These may be considered as characterizing the structure of the matrix.

Now, these odds-ratios may be grouped in order to obtain more understandable information. Let us for instance consider the odds-ratios including the social category $i$, either as an input or as an output category. For perfect mobility, each of these odds-ratios equals 1. If we multiply these quantities together, the result would, in other words, be 1 in the case of perfect mobility. Hence comes the proposal made by Goodman to consider this product as a measure of inheritance in class $i$. A difficulty arises, however, from the fact that the product may also be 1 in situations where we are very far from perfect mobility. Let us consider, for in-

TABLE 2.4

A fictitious mobility matrix

| Fathers' occupational status | Sons' occupational status | | | |
|---|---|---|---|---|
| | 1 | 2 | 3 | Total |
| 1 | 100 | 60 | 50 | 210 |
| 2 | 100 | 120 | 50 | 270 |
| 3 | 40 | 4 | 60 | 104 |
| Total | 240 | 184 | 160 | 584 |

stance, the fictitious matrix of Table 2.4 and call $O_{ij,km}$ the odds-ratio for input categories $i$ and $j$, and output categories $k$ and $m$. The four odds-ratios containing the social category 1 as origin or destination category will be

$$O_{12,12} = (n_{11}/n_{12})/(n_{21}/n_{22}) = (100/60)/(100/120) = 2$$

$$O_{12,13} = (n_{11}/n_{13})/(n_{21}/n_{23}) = (100/50)/(100/50) = 1$$

$$O_{13,13} = (n_{11}/n_{13})/(n_{31}/n_{33}) = (100/50)/(40/60) = 3$$

$$O_{13,12} = (n_{11}/n_{12})/(n_{31}/n_{32}) = (100/60)/(40/4) = 1/6$$

In this case, the product of the four odds-ratios will be 1, although we are clearly not in a situation of perfect mobility.

In spite of these problems the very concept of odds-ratios is certainly a useful one for the analysis of mobility tables. It must, however, be noted that the approach taken by Goodman ignores the now commonly accepted view according to which the marginals of a mobility table should be considered as constraints regulating the mobility processes.

Let us finally briefly evoke another descriptive method, the purpose of which is to provide a rationale for deciding whether two matrices with different marginals may be considered as similar or not*. Let us take a matrix $\mathbf{A}$ with marginals $[a_{(0)i}]$ and $[a_{(1)j}]$ and a matrix $\mathbf{B}$ with marginals $[b_{(0)i}]$ and $[b_{(1)j}]$. These matrices may be mobility tables for two different countries or two different times for the same country. The idea is to transform $\mathbf{A}$ into a matrix, say $\mathbf{A}^0$, with the same marginals as $\mathbf{B}$ and an internal mobility structure identical to that of $\mathbf{A}$.

Let us call $\mathbf{D}_{(0)1}$ a diagonal matrix with elements $b_{(0)i}/a_{(0)i}$ ($i = 1$ to $\sigma$). Then, $\mathbf{D}_{(0)1}\mathbf{A}$ is a matrix with internal mobility structure identical to $\mathbf{A}$ and with the same row totals as $\mathbf{B}$. Then, we want the column marginals of the transformed matrix to be equal to those of $\mathbf{B}$. This is achieved by taking a diagonal matrix $\mathbf{D}_{(1)1}$ with the column totals $b_{(1)i}$ divided by the corresponding column totals of $\mathbf{D}_{(0)}\mathbf{A}$ as elements, and by computing $\mathbf{D}_{(0)1}\mathbf{A}\mathbf{D}_{(1)1}$.

In this latter matrix, the identity with the row totals of $\mathbf{B}$ is, however, destroyed. Then, let us call $\mathbf{D}_{(0)2}$ a diagonal matrix with the row totals of $\mathbf{B}$ respectively divided by the row totals of the

_(handwritten margin notes: "not clear what he means here." "See Manger review p. 322")_

---

* See Deming (1943), Levine (1967), Mosteller (1968) and Tugnault (1970).

previous matrix, $\mathbf{D}_{(0)1}\,\mathbf{A}\mathbf{D}_{(1)1}$, and compute $\mathbf{D}_{(0)2}\mathbf{D}_{(0)1}\,\mathbf{A}\mathbf{D}_{(1)1}$. The row totals of this matrix will be identical with those of $\mathbf{B}$. However, the identity is destroyed for the column totals. Thus, we must continue the iterative process until convergence is sufficient.

# Part 2: Towards a Formal Theory of Social Mobility

# CHAPTER 3

# Theories Without Intervening Variables

## 3.1. Types of theories

We shall now leave the field of measurement and enter the field of theory. We define the concept, theory, very loosely as describing a set of logically interrelated assumptions, some being statements about a given reality which may be true or false or at least plausible or not. If no such statements are present, we speak rather of models, *e.g.* measurement models, than of theories.

In practice, it may, however, sometimes be difficult to distinguish between formal theories and models in this narrow sense. Thus, some of the models analyzed in Chapter 2 may be considered as theories. White's model of Section 2.4 belongs, for instance, to this category. The statement it includes on the existence of two sub-populations, of movers and of stayers, may be considered as a statement describing a reality. The same is true of Goodman's corresponding model. However, in both cases the purpose is to devise an adequate tool for the structural analysis of mobility tables, rather than to test the realism of the distinction between the postulated sub-populations.

In the following development, we shall deal with models, the main aim of which is to provide an adequate representation of mobility processes. In some cases, these models will also provide structural methods for the analysis of mobility tables. But this will be a subsidiary consequence rather than a primary goal.

This second part of the book, on theory, consists of two chapters. In the first, Chapter 3, we deal with models without intervening variables. The Prais Markovian model of Section 2.2 is an example from this class. The model of Blumen *et al.* briefly alluded to in Section 2.4 is another example. In both cases, the only variables introduced are the social positions of the individuals at given times. In the Prais model, the individuals are families and the variables are the social categories to which these individuals belong at each generation. In the original mover—stayer model, the individuals are men and the variables are the social categories to which these men belong at each quarter. However, in some cases, intervening variables are introduced into models of this type. But they are latent variables, *i.e.* unobserved, rather than manifest. The Prais and Blumen models can be contrasted on this point. In the former, all the relations introduced by the model have the form $P(i,j)$ where $i$ stands for the origin category and $j$ for the destination category. In the latter, the relations are rather of the form $P(i, j, k)$ where $i$ and $j$ again describe, respectively, the input and output categories, while $k$ stands for the mover—stayer distinction. But, clearly, $k$ is an unobserved variable. The same is, of course, true for the other versions of the mover—stayer model examined in Chapter 2.

In Chapter 3, we shall survey this class of models characterized either by the absence of intervening variables or by the latent nature of the intervening variables introduced*. In this respect, we must return to provide more details about Blumen's model and then consider the various extensions proposed for this model. One of these extended versions, known as the Cornell Mobility Model, introduces, for instance, a set of relations of the type $P(i,j,d)$ where $i$ and $j$ have the same meaning as above, while $d$ is a new variable $d$, although not exactly latent, is derived from the mobility data rather than from additional information.

belonging to the class we are interested in, since the intervening variable $d$, although not exactly latent, is built from the mobility data rather than from additional information.

The reader may wonder why we have presented White's intergenerational model of Section 2.4 in Chapter 2 and the Cornell model in Chapter 3 since both are, so to speak, intellectual heirs of Blumen's model. The reason for this, again, is that the orientation of the former model is towards the structural analysis of mobility matrices, while that of the latter is towards theory.

In Chapter 4, we deal with models including explicit intervening

---

*The concept of "intervening variable" is used here in a deliberately loose way without explicit reference to casual or temporal ordering.

variables built from some sets of information external to the mobility data themselves, such as differential birth rates, or variables pertaining to the educational system in its relation to social mobility, as well as variables describing shifts in the occupational, or, more broadly, the social structure. We shall present various models proposed by Matras, Bartholomew, Coleman and the present author. We shall not discuss the studies in social mobility which, like Blau and Duncan's study, use general statistical methods rather than models specifically constructed for analyzing social mobility processes. These studies are, so to speak, beyond the scope of this book. Our contention is that, while general statistical methods, such as causal analysis, are probably the easiest way of introducing a sufficient number of intervening variables into the explanation of mobility processes, they also have weaknesses: it is very hard, for instance, to give a precise meaning to the partial correlation coefficient between father's SES and son's educational level, which is a complex consequence depending not only on the inequalities of educational opportunities, but also on the intergenerational changes in the educational and social structures as well as on other factors. Thus, an important strategy certainly worth developing consists in trying to build formal processes embodying those intervening variables that definitely play a role in the generation of mobility processes.

The distinction between models without and with explicit intervening variables, though important, is, of course, but one of the many distinctions which may be introduced. From a mathematical point of view, some mobility models are Markov chains while others are not; some are probabilistic and others algebraic. Some models deal with the moves of individuals, others with moves of jobs; some are macrosociologically oriented, *i.e.* dealing especially with relations between societal variables, others microsociologically oriented, *i.e.* using essentially individual variables. Many other distinctions may be made. But the distinction we choose to stress is possibly the most relevant from a heuristic point of view. When dealing with intragenerational mobility, the introduction of latent intervening variables is certainly a basic strategy. In this case, the information on the positions occupied by a set of individuals may be abundant, since the observations may be repeated at time intervals fairly close to one another. When dealing with intergenerational mobility, the logical context is different. As we have said, perhaps the crucial problem here is to develop, so to speak, a systems analysis approach, *i.e.* to construct a formal theory including the intervening variables, the interaction of which is essential to the explanation of the mobility processes (differential fertility, shifts in the educational structure, shifts in the occupational structure, etc.). Up until now, studies in social mobility have been confronted with a difficult dilemma. Either the models include a sufficient number of intervening variables, but use general statistical instruments, the syntax of which is necessarily poor (for instance, the syntax of causal analysis where the only possible type of statement has the form: the variable $x$ has an influence on the variable $y*$), or they use more sophisticated mathematical models but exclude a number of intervening variables which are essential for the explanation of the mobility processes. This dilemma is generated by the fact that inclusion of a new intervening variable in a statistical model of a general kind does not generally raise any problem, while introduction of a new variable into a stochastic model generally amounts to constructing a new model.

As a consequence of these distinctions, Chapter 3 deals essentially with intragenerational mobility models, while Chapter 4 deals chiefly with intergenerational mobility.

## 3.2. Types of models in the intragenerational case

Ordinary Markov chains represent the simplest type of model used in intragenerational mobility studies. A first extension of this basic model consists, as in the case of Blumen's model, in introducing a latent distinction between stayers and movers, with the assumption that the moves of the movers are regulated by a Markov chain.

One of the axioms of ordinary Markov chains states that the transition matrix is constant, *i.e.* does not change with time. A possible extension of this basic model consists in eliminating this assumption. This may be done in two distinct ways. The first type of extension generates a class of models which we may describe as pseudo-Markovian with collective history. In this case, the assumptions are

---

*More exactly, a difference of $j$ units in a variable $x$ will result, on average, in a difference of $k$ units in variable $y$ at a certain time, certain other specified variables remaining constant. The shortcomings of the casual syntax when dealing with social mobility is much more fully discussed in Boudon (1973b).

(1) that, at a given time, say $t$, the moves of all individuals are regulated by a unique transition matrix, and

(2) that this transition matrix is not fixed, but dependent on time.

The second type of extension produces models which we may call pseudo-Markovian with individual history. These models are characterized by the assumption that the transition matrix which regulates the moves of a given individual is dependent on the moves of this individual in the past. Thus, the moves of a set of individuals with similar individual histories (in a sense which must be defined) will follow a given transition matrix, while the moves of another set of individuals with a different type of individual history will be regulated by another transition matrix.

Another possible type of extension of the basic Markov chain model consists in assuming

(1) that a population is composed of a set of sub-populations,

(2) that each of these sub-populations behaves according to the axioms of a Markov chain, and

(3) that each of these sub-populations is regulated by a different transition matrix.

We shall call these models pseudo-Markovian models with heterogeneous sub-populations.

Finally, mixed models may be constructed by combining some of these extensions. Thus, a model may include both the distinction, stayer—mover, and the collective history assumption. This latter assumption may also be associated with the heterogeneity assumption.

These distinctions are summarized in the tree of Fig. 3.1.

A last distinction which has been stressed by White's (1970a) work remains to be considered. In all the models referred to

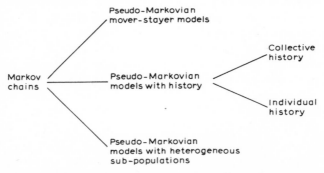

Fig. 3.1. Types of models in the intragenerational case.

above, the initiative in the mobility process belongs to the individuals. They move either as a function only of their current situation, as in the case of ordinary Markov chains, or as a function of their current situation and of some other factors (the history of their past moves, for instance). But no account is taken of occupational opportunities and their possible shifts. In his recent work, White has developed models in which the initiative in the mobility process is granted to the social positions rather than to the individuals. These models analyze the chains of opportunity, as White calls them, that are generated, for instance, by the fact that an individual leaves the occupational system. This leaving generates a process whereby a set of jobs moves from one individual to another.

The attempt made by White in his pioneering work to build models making the moves of the individuals a consequence of structural changes points to a crucial research strategy. Indeed, it is very unlikely that major progress can be made in the direction of building an efficient theory of mobility if the moves of the individuals are not conceived as at least partly dependent on the social structure and its shifts. We shall see in the last chapter that this strategy has been developed, at another level and with a different kind of formalization, in models originally concerned with intergenerational mobility but which may be transformed and refined for intragenerational studies.

At a general level, it is interesting to note that in the field of mobility theory, as in the field of mobility measurement, the sociological quasi-evidence according to which mobility should be considered as depending on the social structures has appeared relatively late in the model-building process.

In the following sections of this chapter, we present some intragenerational models in the order indicated by the tree of Fig. 3.1. In the last section, we shall briefly consider White's opportunity models.

## 3.3. Solution of the original mover—stayer model

We shall first return to the original mover—stayer model, the axioms of which were presented in Section 2.4. As we recall, this model originated from the finding that ordinary Markov chains, when applied to labor turnover, underestimate systematically the number of stayers. Hence arises the idea of creating a latent class of stayers, *i.e.* a sub-population characterized by a degenerate transition matrix (the identity matrix). The problem that gave rise to the mover—stayer model also suggests the other types of extensions of the Markov chains presented in Fig. 3.1. On the other hand, the strategy, adopted by Blumen and his colleagues, of dividing the original population into sub-populations is common to practically all of these pseudo-Markovian models.

As we recall, the basic equation of the mover—stayer model is eqn. (2.53), *viz.*

$$\mathbf{R} = \mathbf{S} + (\mathbf{I} - \mathbf{S})\mathbf{M} \tag{3.1}$$

where $\mathbf{R} = [r_{ij}]$ is the observed transition matrix corresponding to a short time unit (a quarter in Blumen's original study); while $\mathbf{S} = \mathrm{diag}[s_i]$ is a diagonal matrix giving the proportion of stayers in each occupational category and $\mathbf{M} = [m_{ij}]$ is the transition matrix describing the transition rates of the movers. $\mathbf{I}$ is, of course, the identity matrix.

In White's version of this model (Section 2.4), the solution was obtained by assuming a perfect mobility pattern. But this assumption was introduced primarily because of the special problems raised by the application of the model to intergenerational mobility. In the intragenerational case, data on successive quarters are available, so that a different strategy may be used.

The movers are assumed to move according to an ordinary homogeneous Markov chain: the transition matrix $\mathbf{M}$ is not time-dependent and the moves between, say, $t$ and $(t + 1)$ depend only on the position at $t$. Considering the entire population, let us call $\mathbf{R}^{(1)}$ the transition matrix for the time interval between the beginning of the initial quarter 0 and the beginning of the following quarter 1; $\mathbf{R}^{(2)}$ the transition matrix between the beginning of quarter 0 and of quarter 2; ...; $\mathbf{R}^{(k)}$ the transition matrix between the beginning of quarter 0 and of quarter $k$. Then, by the assumptions

$$\mathbf{R}^{(1)} = \mathbf{S} + (\mathbf{I} - \mathbf{S})\mathbf{M} \tag{3.2a}$$

$$\mathbf{R}^{(2)} = \mathbf{S} + (\mathbf{I} - \mathbf{S})\mathbf{M}^2 \tag{3.2b}$$

$$\cdots\cdots\cdots\cdots\cdots\cdots\cdots$$

$$\mathbf{R}^{(k)} = \mathbf{S} + (\mathbf{I} - \mathbf{S})\mathbf{M}^k \tag{3.2c}$$

And in the limit (see Section 2.2)

$$\mathbf{R}^* = \mathbf{S} + (\mathbf{I} - \mathbf{S})\mathbf{M}^* \tag{3.3}$$

where $\mathbf{M}^*$ is the equilibrium transition matrix, *i.e.* a matrix with all its rows equal so that $m_{ij}^*$ may simply be written $m_j^*$.

Let us now suppose the turnover data between the beginning of the initial quarter and the beginning of some quarter $k$, sufficiently removed in time, are available. Then

$$\mathbf{R}^{(k)} \sim \mathbf{S} + (\mathbf{I} - \mathbf{S})\mathbf{M}^* \qquad (k \text{ great}) \qquad (3.4)$$

or, in ordinary non-matrix notation

$$r_{ij}^{(k)} \sim (1 - s_i)m_{ij}^* \qquad (i \neq j) \qquad (3.5a)$$

$$r_{ii}^{(k)} \sim s_i + (1 - s_i)m_{ii}^* \qquad (3.5b)$$

Or, since $\mathbf{M}^*$ has all its rows equal

$$r_{ij}^{(k)} \sim (1 - s_i)m_j^* \qquad (i \neq j) \qquad (3.5c)$$

$$r_{ij}^{(k)} \sim s_i + (1 - s_i)m_i^* \qquad (3.5d)$$

Now, using eqn. (3.5) a solution may be derived for the unknown parameters. Indeed

$$\frac{r_{ij}^{(k)}}{\sum\limits_{j \neq i} r_{ij}^{(k)}} = \frac{(1 - s_i)m_{ij}^*}{(1 - s_i) \sum\limits_{j \neq i} m_{ij}^*}$$

$$= \frac{m_{ij}^*}{\sum\limits_{j \neq i} m_{ij}^*} = \frac{m_j^*}{\sum\limits_{j \neq i} m_j^*} \qquad (3.6)$$

By combining appropriate sets of equations similar to eqn. (3.6), linear systems are derived which may be easily solved for $m_j^*$ values. We shall ignore here, as usual, the statistical estimation problem raised by the fact that there are several solutions according to the way the equations are combined, and refer the reader on this point to the statistical appendix. Once the $m_j^*$ values have been determined, the next step is to introduce them into eqn. (3.3) and to solve eqn. (3.3) for the values of $s_i$. The final step is to estimate the values of $m_{ij}$, the elements of $\mathbf{M}$. This is readily done using eqn. (3.2a).

In their original study, Blumen and his colleagues used $k = 8$, *i.e.* they used, for the estimation of the $m_j^*$'s, the observed transition matrix corresponding to a time interval of 8 quarters. The fit between the observed matrix $R^{(8)}$ and the corresponding theoretical matrix reproduced by using the estimates of the parameters was good, while it was poor for $R^{(4)}$ and $R^{(11)}$. Using the estimated values of the parameters to reproduce $R^{(4)}$ and $R^{(11)}$ led respectively to an underestimation and to an overestimation of the diagonal cells.

This means that the mover—stayer distinction does not lead to an adequate representation of the analyzed mobility process. The main interest of Blumen's model actually lies in the general pseudo-Markovian strategy it points to more than in the particular realization of this strategy it presents.

Blumen and his colleagues have also proposed a more sophisticated version of the original mover—stayer model. In this version, a quarter is assumed to be divided into an arbitrary number of smaller time units, say $m$. There are $(m + 1)$ categories of people: those who are stayers in all intervals, those who are stayers in all but 1, in all but 2, etc. intervals. The moves over one quarter are then regulated by the identity matrix $I$ for the stayers in all intervals, by a matrix $M$ for the stayers in all but one interval, by $M^2$ for the stayers in all but 2 intervals,..., by $M^m$ for those who were movers in all $m$ intervals. By assuming $m$ to be very large, these axioms generate a model, the equations of which can be solved for the unknown parameters.

### 3.4. Pseudo-Markovian models with collective history

Another strategy which may be used in order to meet the problem raised by the underestimation of the diagonal cells generated by ordinary Markov chains consists in making the transition matrix time-variable, *i.e.* in relaxing the stationarity assumption of ordinary Markov chains.

*A general model with collective history*

This model rests on the assumption that, as time elapses, people want to find a resting place. In other words, job mobility is pictured as a trial-and-error process. In the first stages, people are likely to try to change their occupational position in order to obtain a better one. If they reach a better position, their likelihood of change will decrease. If they do not reach a better position, their propensity to change will also decrease. Thus, as the trial-and-error process continues, the probability of a new move is assumed to decrease. In order to make this a collective history model, either we may suppose that we are dealing with a cohort, *i.e.* with a set of people all of whose lengths of exposure to the trial-and-error process is the same or nearly the same, or we may suppose that the population is composed of a mixture of different cohorts. As time elapses, the length of exposure to the trial-and-error process, of course, increases for all cohorts, so that with mixed cohorts, also, the probability of moving should decrease. It should be noted that these assumptions do not take account of the individual histories. They simply formalize the idea that, as time elapses, everybody is growing older, *i.e.* is likely to be closer to an equilibrium position in the trial-and-error process of job selection. Again, it must be noted that this model, like most intragenerational models, ignores the structural conditions which certainly have an effect on the mobility processes. Thus, we shall assume that the transition matrix $\mathbf{R}$ is a function of time and call it $\mathbf{R}_t$.

There are, of course, many ways of making $\mathbf{R}$ a function of time. One way would be to assume that all values of $r_{ij}$ $(i = j)$ decrease according to the same function of time. Conversely, one might suppose that this decrease is a function of time, but also of $i$, the origin category, and of $j$, the destination category. One might, for instance, assume that the decrease in probability of going from $i$ to $j$ is greater the greater the distance between $i$ and $j$. An intermediate strategy would be to assume that the probability of moving from $i$ to $j$ is a function of time and of $i$, the origin category. This intermediate assumption is both perhaps realistic and undoubtedly simpler than the previous one: it supposes that, in general, the propensity for an individual to leave his current position will decrease, but that this decrease may be different according to the nature of this current position. It supposes, in other words, that the propensity to leave is regulated both by the more or less appealing character of the current situation and by the time elapsed since the beginning of the trial-and-error process.

Since the decrease in the propensity to leave is assumed not to be dependent on the destination category, an alternative way of describing the basic assumption of the model is to make the probability of staying, say, in category $i$, a function of time and of $i$.

In particular, let us suppose that the diagonal element $r_{(t)ii}$ of $\mathbf{R}_t$ is increased each time by a constant multiple $x_i$ $(x_i \geqslant 0)$. Since the sum would then be $1 + r_{(t)ii}x_i$, the entire row must be normalized by dividing through by that sum. This model thus states that

$$r_{(t+1)ii} = (r_{(t)ii} + r_{(t)ii}x_i)/(1 + r_{(t)ii}x_i) \tag{3.7a}$$

$$r_{(t+1)ij} = r_{(t)ij}/(1 + r_{(t)ii}x_i) \qquad i \neq j \tag{3.7b}$$

For convenience, we let

$$k_{(t)i} = \frac{1}{1 + x_i r_{(t)ii}} \tag{3.8}$$

Let $D_t = \text{diag}[r(t)_{ii}]$ be a diagonal matrix including the diagonal elements of $R_t = [r_{(t)ij}]$, the transition matrix at time $t$. On the other hand, let $X = \text{diag}[x_i]$ and $K_t = \text{diag}[k_{(t)i}]$ both be diagonal matrices. Then we can see from the definitions that

$$R_{(t+1)} = K_t(R_t + D_t X) \tag{3.9}$$

or explicitly,

$$
\begin{bmatrix}
r_{(t+1)11} & r_{(t+1)12} & \cdots & r_{(t+1)1\sigma} \\
r_{(t+1)21} & r_{(t+1)22} & \cdots & r_{(t+1)2\sigma} \\
\cdots & \cdots & \cdots & \cdots \\
r_{(t+1)\sigma 1} & r_{(t+1)\sigma 2} & \cdots & r_{(t+1)\sigma\sigma}
\end{bmatrix}
$$

$$
=
\begin{bmatrix}
k_{(t)1} & 0 & \cdots & 0 \\
0 & k_{(t)2} & \cdots & 0 \\
\cdots & \cdots & \cdots & \cdots \\
0 & 0 & & k_{(t)}
\end{bmatrix}
\left\{
\begin{bmatrix}
r_{(t)11} & r_{(t)12} & \cdots & r_{(t)1\sigma} \\
r_{(t)21} & r_{(t)22} & \cdots & r_{(t)2\sigma} \\
\cdots & \cdots & \cdots & \cdots \\
r_{(t)\sigma 1} & r_{(t)\sigma 2} & \cdots & r_{(t)\sigma\sigma}
\end{bmatrix}
\right.
$$

$$
+
\begin{bmatrix}
r_{(t)11} & 0 & \cdots & 0 \\
0 & r_{(t)22} & \cdots & 0 \\
\cdots & \cdots & \cdots & \cdots \\
0 & 0 & \cdots & r_{(t)\sigma\sigma}
\end{bmatrix}
\begin{bmatrix}
x_1 & 0 & \cdots & 0 \\
0 & x_2 & \cdots & 0 \\
\cdots & \cdots & \cdots & \cdots \\
0 & 0 & \cdots & x_\sigma
\end{bmatrix}
\left.
\vphantom{\begin{bmatrix} 1 \\ 1 \\ 1 \\ 1 \end{bmatrix}}
\right\} \tag{3.10}
$$

A first use of the model for data analogous to Blumen's (turn-over tables for a number of successive time units) would be to ascertain whether it predicts the process correctly or not. Thus, suppose we have data for $n$ successive quarters and take the turn-over tables corresponding respectively to the beginning and to the end of the first and of the second quarters. Then, by eqn. (3.9)

$$r_{(t+1)ij} = \frac{r_{(t)ij}}{1 + r_{(t)ii}x_i} \qquad (i \neq j) \qquad (3.11a)$$

$$r_{(t+1)ii} = \frac{r_{(t)ii} + r_{(t)ii}x_i}{1 + r_{(t)ii}x_i} \qquad (3.11b)$$

These equations are linear and may be solved for the $x$'s. The next step would be to verify that these estimates generate a good fit in predicting the turnover tables for the following quarters.

The transition matrix between the beginning of the first quarter and the beginning of, say, the $t$th quarter will be, for this model

$$\mathbf{R}^{(t)} = \mathbf{R}_1 \mathbf{R}_2 \dots \mathbf{R}_t \qquad (3.12)$$

Provided the elements of $\mathbf{X}$ are all positive, the limit of $\mathbf{R}_t$ is

$$\lim_t \mathbf{R}_t = \mathbf{I} \qquad (3.13)$$

Thus, since

$$\mathbf{P}_{(t+1)} = \mathbf{P}_t \mathbf{R}_{(t+1)}, \qquad \mathbf{P}_{(t+1)} \sim \mathbf{P}_t \qquad (3.14)$$

for large values of $t$. This shows that the model generates, as do ordinary Markov chains, an equilibrium distribution (which of course will be different from the Markov chain equilibrium). Equation (3.14) would also hold if $\mathbf{X}$, instead of being assumed constant, were supposed to be a function of time. We could, for instance, suppose

$$\mathbf{X}_t = \text{diag}[x_{(t)i}] = \text{diag}[x_i^t] \qquad (0 < x_i < 1) \qquad (3.15)$$

With eqn. (3.15), the change in $r_{(t)ii}$ would be made decreasing with time.

83

## Possible variations of the model

Of course, there are as many possible variations of the model as there are possible assumptions for $\mathbf{X}$. $\mathbf{X}$ may be made a scalar matrix, the elements of which would be then independent of the origin categories. A model of this type was proposed by Mayer (1967, 1968).

Another interesting suggestion, also proposed by Mayer, is to use pseudo-cohort versions of this kind of model with collective history. Suppose we have a given population which we may separate into sub-populations more homogeneous in age and then expose separately to the pseudo-Markovian process described above. Let $\mathbf{M}_0(i) = \text{diag}[m_{(0)ij}]$ be a diagonal matrix describing the proportion of these people in social category $j$ at time 0 belonging to the age group $i$. Then the assumptions of this pseudo-cohort version of the general collective history model lead to

$$\mathbf{R}_1 = \mathbf{M}_0(1)\mathbf{K}_0(1)[\mathbf{R}_0(1) + \mathbf{D}_0(1)\mathbf{X}(1)] + \ldots$$
$$+ \mathbf{M}_0(g)\mathbf{K}_0[(g)\mathbf{R}_0(g) + \mathbf{D}_0(g)\mathbf{X}(g)] \qquad (3.16)$$

where the numbers 1 to $g$ indicate that the matrices $\mathbf{K}$, $\mathbf{R}$, $\mathbf{D}$ and $\mathbf{X}$ are now defined on each of the $g$ age groups. Generally

$$\mathbf{R}_{(t+1)} = \mathbf{M}_t(1)\mathbf{K}_t(1)[\mathbf{R}_t(1) + \mathbf{D}_t(1)\mathbf{X}(1)] + \ldots$$
$$+ \mathbf{M}_t(g)\mathbf{K}_t(g)[\mathbf{R}_t(g) + \mathbf{D}_t(g)\mathbf{X}(g)] \qquad (3.17)$$

It must be stated finally that, as McFarland (1970) rightly points out, these models with collective history are, so to speak, an ad hoc answer to the problem raised by the failure of ordinary Markov chains to predict the correct amount of job stability over time. Since the ordinary Markov chains underestimate the stability, an obvious temptation is to build the trend towards stability into the model. However, this criticism applies to the mover—stayer models as well as to the models with collective or individual history.

Like the mover—stayer models, the models with collective history have another common weakness: they make all individuals similar provided they belong to the same latent class (mover—stayer models) or to the same age group (pseudo-cohort model with collective history). In this respect, the Cornell Mobility Model, which

84

makes the moves of an individual dependent on the pattern of his previous moves, may undoubtedly be considered as a major step forward.

## 3.5. A class of pseudo-Markovian models with individual history

The Cornell Mobility Model* introduces individual history in the form of the axiom of cumulative inertia. This axiom states that the longer an individual has remained in a given occupational position, the more likely he will be to stay in this category at the next step. In the models with collective history, the trend towards inertia was considered to be similar for all individuals, or for all individuals of the same age, or for all individuals of the same age and origin category, according to the version of the model. Here, the trend towards inertia is, at each step, similar for the individuals who, in some sense which must be defined, have the same individual history of past moves. Thus, the sub-class of people who have already stayed in their occupational position for, say, 5 consecutive time periods will be considered as less likely to move at the next step than those who have stayed in the same position during, say, 2 time periods.

The axiom of cumulative inertia is certainly of great relevance when dealing with social phenomena. It is almost obvious that, in general, the longer an individual stays in a given state, the less likely he will be to move: the longer a criminal career, the greater the probability of a new crime; the greater the number of publications, the more likely a new publication, etc.

*Some possible versions of the axiom of cumulative inertia*

The process generated by the Cornell Mobility Model starts exactly like a Markov chain. Let the row vector $\mathbf{p}_0$ describe the distribution of the population in the various social categories at time 0.

$$\mathbf{p}_0 = [p_{(0)i}] \tag{3.18}$$

At the next step, this population moves according to a transition

---

* See Ginsberg (1971), Henry (1971), Henry *et al.* (1971) and McGinnis (1968).

matrix $R(0) = [r_{ij}{}^{(0)}]$. A new distribution, $p_1$, results

$$p_1 = p_0 R(0) \tag{3.19}$$

At this point, the Markov chain process is altered: we distinguish two sub-classes of people, those who stayed in the same social position at time 0 and at time 1, and those who have moved. Let us call $p_1{}^1 = [p_{(1)i}{}^1]$ the row vector describing the proportions of those who, at time 1, stayed once and $p_1{}^0 = [p_{(1)i}{}^0]$ the row vector describing the proportions of those who, at time 1, did not stay, or stayed 0 times. Of course

$$p_1 = p_1{}^1 + p_1{}^0 \tag{3.20}$$

and

$$p_1{}^1 = p_0 D(0) \tag{3.21}$$

where $D(0)$ is a diagonal matrix containing the diagonal elements of $R(0)$, while

$$p_1{}^0 = p_0 [R(0) - D(0)] \tag{3.22}$$

The next step introduces the axiom of cumulative inertia. We suppose that those who moved will move again according to $R(0)$, while those who stayed will move according to $R(1)$, a matrix with diagonal elements greater than those of $R(0)$. Thus $R(0)$ is the transition matrix regulating the moves of the people who have stayed 0 times, while $R(1)$ is the transition matrix regulating the moves of those who have stayed once. So, the movers go on moving according to a Markov chain, while the others are regulated by a different type of process.

With these assumptions, the distribution at time 2 is

$$p_2 = p_1{}^1 R(1) + p_1{}^0 R(0) \tag{3.23}$$

or, substituting eqns. (3.21) and (3.22)

$$p_2 = p_0 D(0) R(1) + p_0 [R(0) - D(0)] R(0)$$

$$= p_0 \{ D(0) R(1) + [R(0) - D(0)] R(0) \} \tag{3.24}$$

With respect to their individual history, we have at this step four categories of people: the stayer-stayers, the mover-stayers, the stayer-movers and the mover-movers. Generally, at time $t$, the process will generate $2^t$ sub-classes of people, since, at each time, people may either move or stay. Then, $t$ time units will generate $2^t$ distinct types of careers.

Since we are interested in the effect of stability on the probability of a next move, it is pointless to consider these $2^t$ patterns separately. They have to be grouped into equivalence classes.

At this point, several distinct decisions may be taken in order to give the axiom of cumulative inertia a precise form.

*Form A of the cumulative inertia axiom.* Consider an individual who stays once: he will move at the next step according to $R(1)$. If he stays again, he will move at the following step according to $R(2)$, a matrix with diagonal figures greater than those of $R(1)$. Suppose now that he has stayed twice (times 1 and 2) and moves at the next step (time 3). Then, in form A of the axiom, at time 4, his moves will be regulated by $R(0)$. In this form of the axiom, the stability is recorded at a given time, say $t$, only when the individual did not move during a number of consecutive time periods immediately preceding $t$. If a stability period is interrupted by a move, its effect is, so to speak, erased, and the next moves are regulated by $R(0)$.

*Form B of the cumulative inertia axiom.* In this case, a stability period is recorded, even if interrupted by a move. Let us take again an individual who stayed at times 1 and 2. At time 0, his move was regulated by $R(0)$ as was everyone's; at time 1, it was regulated by $R(1)$, at time 2 by $R(2)$. Suppose, now, he appears as a mover at time 3. Then, at time 4, his move will be regulated by $R(2)$ in form B of the cumulative inertia axiom. In other words, with this form of the axiom, a stability period is recorded, even if it is interrupted. The effect of this interruption is that the further moves of our individual (or, more exactly of the sub-class of individuals to which he belongs) will all be regulated by $R(2)$ until a new stability period appears.

*Form C of the cumulative inertia axiom.* Form A of the axiom corresponds to a system without memory: as soon as a stability period is interrupted, its record is erased. Form B corresponds to a system with, say, a rigid form of memory: it is able to remember but not to forget. In form C, the system is able both to remember and to forget. Let us again consider a sub-class of individuals who have stayed twice and then moved at the following step. Their moves have been regulated respectively by $R(0)$, $R(1)$, $R(2)$, $R(3)$ at times 0, 1, 2 and 3, as in form B of the axiom. But let us suppose a further move comes next. Then, according to form C of the axiom, the memory of the stability period will decrease: the

| Pattern | Form of the axiom | Time | | | | | | | |
|---------|-------------------|------|---|---|---|---|---|---|---|
| | | 0 | 1 | 2 | 3 | 4 | 5 | 6 | 7 |
| 1 | | $1 \to 1 \to 1 \to 2 \to 2 \to 2 \to 1 \to 2$ | | | | | | | |
| | A | $R(0)$ $R(1)$ $R(2)$ $R(0)$ $R(1)$ $R(2)$ $R(0)$ $R(0)$ | | | | | | | |
| | B | $R(0)$ $R(1)$ $R(2)$ $R(2)$ $R(3)$ $R(4)$ $R(4)$ $R(4)$ | | | | | | | |
| | C | $R(0)$ $R(1)$ $R(2)$ $R(2)$ $R(3)$ $R(4)$ $R(4)$ $R(3)$ | | | | | | | |
| 2 | | $1 \to 1 \to 1 \to 2 \to 1 \to 2 \to 1 \to 1$ | | | | | | | |
| | A | $R(0)$ $R(1)$ $R(2)$ $R(0)$ $R(0)$ $R(0)$ $R(0)$ $R(1)$ | | | | | | | |
| | B | $R(0)$ $R(1)$ $R(2)$ $R(2)$ $R(2)$ $R(2)$ $R(2)$ $R(3)$ | | | | | | | |
| | C | $R(0)$ $R(1)$ $R(2)$ $R(2)$ $R(1)$ $R(0)$ $R(0)$ $R(1)$ | | | | | | | |

Fig. 3.2. Successive transition matrices regulating the moves of two sub-classes of people showing the move patterns 1 and 2 as a function of the form of the cumulative inertia axiom.

regulation will follow $R(1)$ and eventually $R(0)$ if the following step is again characterized by a move.

These three forms of the axiom of cumulative inertia are illustrated in Fig. 3.2. We suppose, in this figure, two possible social categories numbered 1 and 2, and consider two possible patterns of moves. The figure gives the transition matrices which are applied to the sub-classes characterized respectively by these two patterns as a function of the form taken by the axiom of cumulative inertia.

In the original presentation of the Cornell Mobility Model by McGinnis (1968), form A of the axiom was used. In the following presentation, we shall instead use form B, which seems to be more realistic, without leading to the complications of C.

*Version B of the Cornell Mobility Model*

Let us return to eqn. (3.24). As mentioned, $p_2$ includes four sub-classes: those who have stayed or have moved twice, those who have stayed and then moved, those who have moved and then stayed. If we use form B of the axiom of cumulative inertia, these two latter sub-classes will be treated as indistinct. Both will be regulated by $R(1)$ at the next step, while the moves of the twice-stayers will be regulated by $R(2)$, and those of the twice-movers by $R(0)$. We shall have, in other words

$$\mathbf{p}_2 = \mathbf{p}_2{}^2 + \mathbf{p}_2{}^1 + \mathbf{p}_2{}^0 \tag{3.25}$$

where $\mathbf{p}_2{}^2$ is a row vector describing the twice-stayers at time 2, $\mathbf{p}_2{}^1$ the row vector of the once stayers at time 2, and $\mathbf{p}_2{}^0$ the row-vector of those who stayed 0 times. Of course

$$\mathbf{p}_2{}^2 = \mathbf{p}_0 D(0)D(1) \tag{3.26}$$

And, $\mathbf{p}_2{}^1$ is a sum of two components: a component corresponding to those who stayed and moved, *i.e.* $\mathbf{p}_0 D(0)[R(1) - D(1)]$, and a component corresponding to those who moved and stayed, *i.e.* $\mathbf{p}_0 [R(0) - D(0)] D(1)$

$$\mathbf{p}_2{}^1 = \mathbf{p}_0 D(0)[R(1) - D(1)] + \mathbf{p}_0 [R(0) - D(0)] D(0) \tag{3.27}$$

Finally

$$\mathbf{p}_2{}^0 = \mathbf{p}_0 [R(0) - D(0)] [R(0) - D(0)] \tag{3.28}$$

According to the axiom of cumulative inertia (form B), the distribution at time 3 will be

$$\mathbf{p}_3 = \mathbf{p}_2{}^2 R(2) + \mathbf{p}_2{}^1 R(1) + \mathbf{p}_2{}^0 R(0) \tag{3.29}$$

or, substituting eqns. $(3.26)-(3.28)$ into eqn. $(3.29)$

$$\mathbf{p}_3 = \mathbf{p}_0 D(0)D(1)R(2) + \mathbf{p}_0 D(0)[R(1) - D(1)] R(1)$$

$$+ \mathbf{p}_0 [R(0) - D(0)] D(0)R(1)$$

$$+ \mathbf{p}_0 [R(0) - D(0)] [R(0) - D(0)] R(0) \tag{3.30}$$

At the next step, we must consider separately the $2^3$ sub-classes of which $\mathbf{p}_3$ is the sum, and regroup these into four equivalence classes corresponding respectively to those who have stayed 0, 1, 2 or 3 times. We then have, for the 3-times stayers at time 3

$$\mathbf{p}_3{}^3 = \mathbf{p}_0 D(0)D(1)D(2) \tag{3.31}$$

for the twice-stayers at time 3

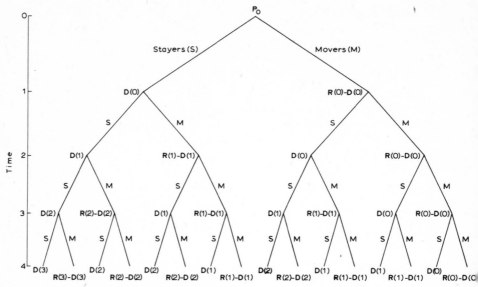

Fig. 3.3. Graph of the Cornell model (version B). The product of the quantities met by going down a path of the tree gives the distribution at time $t$ of individuals who have followed the corresponding pattern.

$$\mathbf{p}_3{}^2 = \mathbf{p}_0 \mathbf{D}(0)[\mathbf{R}(1) - \mathbf{D}(1)]\mathbf{D}(1)$$

$$+ \mathbf{p}_0 [\mathbf{R}(0) - \mathbf{D}(0)]\mathbf{D}(1)\mathbf{D}(1)$$

$$+ \mathbf{p}_0 \mathbf{D}(0)\mathbf{D}(1)[\mathbf{R}(2) - \mathbf{D}(2)] \qquad (3.32)$$

etc.

In order to visualize the process, the graph in Fig. 3.3 may be useful. At each time, the tree is divided into two branches. The left branch describes the stayers, while the right branch describes the movers. The distribution corresponding to a given pattern of moves is obtained by multiplying, following the temporal order, the quantities which appear at the appropriate crossing points. Thus, the distribution of the stayers at time 1 is given by $\mathbf{p}_0 \mathbf{D}(0)$; the distribution of those who stayed at time 1 and move at time 2 by $\mathbf{p}_0 \mathbf{D}(0)[\mathbf{R}(1) - \mathbf{D}(1)]$; the distribution of those who moved at times 1, 2 and 3 by $\mathbf{p}_0 [\mathbf{R}(0) - \mathbf{D}(0)]^3$, etc. It is readily verified that this representation is in agreement with eqns. (3.21), (3.22), (3.26)—(3.28), (3.31) and (3.32).

The overall distribution at a given time is obtained by adding the products corresponding to the terminal points of the tree at that time. Thus,

90

$$\mathbf{p}_0 \mathbf{D}(0) \{\mathbf{D}(1) + [\mathbf{R}(1) - \mathbf{D}(1)]\} + \mathbf{p}_0 [\mathbf{R}(0) - \mathbf{D}(0)]$$

$$\times \{\mathbf{D}(0) + [\mathbf{R}(0) - \mathbf{D}(0)]\}$$

$$= \mathbf{p}_0 \mathbf{D}(0) \mathbf{R}(1) + \mathbf{p}_0 [\mathbf{R}(0) - \mathbf{D}(0)] \mathbf{R}(0) = \mathbf{p}_2 \qquad (3.33)$$

This verifies that eqn. (3.33) is indeed similar to eqn. (3.24).

Let us note, incidentally, that this tree representation may also be used when form A of the cumulative inertia axiom is preferred. The only difference is that all the matrices located below a $\mathbf{R}(x) - \mathbf{D}(x)$ matrix are $\mathbf{D}(0)$ on the left branch and $\mathbf{R}(0) - \mathbf{D}(0)$ on the right branch. The tree representation can, of course, also be used when the inertia axiom takes form C.

*Uses of the model*

Let us suppose we have at our disposal a set of turnover data for say, $n$ quarters, as in the case of Blumen's model. One way of using the Cornell model is to interpret the transition matrix corresponding to the first two quarters as $\mathbf{R}(0)$. $\mathbf{D}(0)$ will be the diagonal matrix including the diagonal elements of $\mathbf{R}(0)$. Now, by eqn. (3.33), the transition matrix corresponding to the turnover between quarter 0 and quarter 2, say $\mathbf{R}^{(2)}$, is

$$\mathbf{R}^{(2)} = \mathbf{D}(0) \mathbf{R}(1) + [\mathbf{R}(0) - \mathbf{D}(0)] \mathbf{R}(0) \qquad (3.34)$$

This equation can be solved for $\mathbf{R}(1)$, *i.e.* the transition matrix regulating the moves at quarter 2 of those who kept the same position at quarters 0 and 1. Indeed, we draw from eqn. (3.34)

$$\mathbf{R}(1) = \mathbf{D}(0)^{-1} \{\mathbf{R}^{(2)} - [\mathbf{R}(0) - \mathbf{D}(0)] \mathbf{R}(0)\} \qquad (3.35)$$

The question is then whether $\mathbf{R}(1)$, when compared with $\mathbf{R}(0)$, actually fits the assumption of the Cornell model. In other words are the diagonal elements of $\mathbf{R}(1)$ larger than those of $\mathbf{R}(0)$? It is possible to continue in this way, and estimate successively $\mathbf{R}(2)$, $\mathbf{R}(3)$, etc.

In his original paper, McGinnis was concerned with the theoretical analysis of the Cornell model rather than with its application to empirical data. He used a simulation procedure to explore the behavior of the model (with the A version of the inertia axiom), analyzing the limiting distribution $\lim \mathbf{p}_t$ as well as the limiting values of the diagonal elements of $\lim_t \mathbf{R}^{(t)}$ the gross transition matrix between quarters 0 and $t$.

91

The Cornell model is obviously complicated. Its theoretical analysis is not simple. McGinnis has shown, however, that when the inertia axiom takes form A, a distribution vector $\mathbf{p}^*$ exists such that $\lim_t \mathbf{p}_t \to \mathbf{p}^*$. Of course, this limiting distribution will be different from the limiting distribution of a Markov chain. Let us only mention that, according to the simulation experiments conducted by McGinnis, this limiting distribution may, under given conditions, be dependent on the initial distribution. This contrasts the Cornell model with Markov chains.

The proof of the existence of a limiting vector $\mathbf{p}^*$ is not given by McGinnis in his paper. In the following sub-section, we give a proof for the version of the model considered here (cumulative inertia axiom of type B), rather than for that originally considered by McGinnis.

*The convergence of $\mathbf{p}_t$ towards a limiting distribution*

The proof of the existence of a limiting distribution $\mathbf{p}^*$ may be given as follows. Let us take $t$ to be very large. The row vector $\mathbf{p}_t$ giving the distribution of the population at $t$ may be analyzed into the sum of $2^t$ components corresponding to each of the $2^t$ possible moving-staying patterns between time 0 and time $t$. Number these patterns from 1 to $2^t$.

$$\mathbf{p}_t = \mathbf{p}_t^{\,1} + \mathbf{p}_t^{\,2} + \dots + \mathbf{p}_t^{\,2^t} \tag{3.36}$$

Consider now $\mathbf{p}_t^{\,1}$ and suppose it concerns the people who have always stayed from time 0 to time $t$. Using the tree of Fig. 3.3, it is readily verified that

$$\mathbf{p}_t^{\,1} = \mathbf{p}_0 \mathbf{D}(0)\mathbf{D}(1)\mathbf{D}(2) \dots \mathbf{D}(t-1) \tag{3.37}$$

At $(t+1)$, we have

$$\mathbf{P}_{(t+1)}^{\,1} = \mathbf{p}_0 \mathbf{D}(0)\mathbf{D}(1)\mathbf{D}(2) \dots \mathbf{D}(t-1)\mathbf{R}(t)$$

$$= \mathbf{p}_t^{\,1} \mathbf{R}(t) \tag{3.38}$$

But, by the assumptions of the model

$$\lim \mathbf{R}(t) = \lim \mathbf{D}(t) = \mathbf{I} \tag{3.39}$$

Thus, in the limit,

$$\mathbf{P}_{(t+1)}^{\,1} = \mathbf{p}_t^{\,1} \tag{3.40}$$

Practically, we shall suppose $t$ great enough so that

$$\mathbf{R}(t) \sim \mathbf{I} \tag{3.41}$$

Let us now consider the sub-vector $\mathbf{p}_t{}^2$ and suppose it concerns the sub-class of people who moved between time 0 and time 1 and then stayed the rest of the time.

$$\mathbf{p}_t{}^2 = \mathbf{p}_0 [\mathbf{R}(0) - \mathbf{D}(0)] \mathbf{D}(0)\mathbf{D}(1) \dots \mathbf{D}(t-2) \tag{3.42}$$

In order to show that $\mathbf{p}_t{}^2$ converges towards a limit, we may consider the process at time $(t+1)$ rather than $t$. Then

$$\mathbf{p}_{(t+1)}{}^2 = \mathbf{p}_0 [\mathbf{R}(0) - \mathbf{D}(0)] \mathbf{D}(0)\mathbf{D}(1) \dots \mathbf{D}(t-1) \tag{3.43}$$

An argument similar to that used for eqn. (3.38) shows then that $\mathbf{p}_{(t+1)}{}^2$ converges towards a limit. Indeed

$$\mathbf{p}_{(t+2)}{}^2 = \mathbf{p}_0 [\mathbf{R}(0) - \mathbf{D}(0)] \mathbf{D}(0)\mathbf{D}(1) \dots \mathbf{D}(t-1)\mathbf{R}(t) \tag{3.44}$$

so that, from eqn. (3.41)

$$\mathbf{p}_{(t+2)}{}^2 \sim \mathbf{p}_{(t+1)}{}^2 \tag{3.45}$$

Now consider the sub-class, say, $i$ of people who always stayed except in the last time period

$$\mathbf{p}_t{}^i = \mathbf{p}_0 \mathbf{D}(0)\mathbf{D}(1) \dots \mathbf{D}(t-2)[\mathbf{R}(t-2) - \mathbf{D}(t-2)] \tag{3.46}$$

An argument exactly similar to the previous one shows that if we consider the process at $(t+1)$, from eqn. (3.41), we have

$$\mathbf{p}_{(t+2)}{}^i \sim \mathbf{p}_{(t+1)}{}^i \tag{3.47}$$

Generally, a similar argument applied to all the possibilities shows that all the sub-vectors describing the people that have moved just once, at any time, will converge towards a limiting distribution.

Now, it is obvious that we cannot simply continue in this way, since going from $t$ to $(t+1)$ has the effect of replacing the vector $\mathbf{p}_t$ which is a sum of $2^t$ components by the vector $\mathbf{p}_{(t+1)}$ which is a sum of $2^{(t+1)}$ components. When we show that a class of vectors converges, we also create new classes of vectors which must also be shown to converge.

In order to escape from this dilemma, let us group the sub-vectors $\mathbf{p}_t{}^1$, $\mathbf{p}_t{}^2$, ... into classes defined by the number of moves. In the class 0, we place the unique sub-vector corresponding to those who have stayed all the time in class 1, the vectors corresponding to those who always have stayed every time except once, etc. Previously, we showed that the sub-vectors belonging to the classes 0 and 1 all converge towards a limiting distribution. But, by extending the process to $(t+1)$, we created a new class of sub-vectors, since the classes which were numbered from 0 to $t$ must now be numbered from 0 to $(t+1)$.

Let us call $\mathbf{q}_t^0, \mathbf{q}_t^1, ..., \mathbf{q}_t^t$ the sets of vectors corresponding respectively to the $(t + 1)$ classes which may be distinguished at time $t$. Then we have shown that all the elements of $\mathbf{q}_t^0$ and of $\mathbf{q}_{(t+1)}^1$ converge towards a limit. But the previous argument can easily be extended and shows generally that all the elements of $\mathbf{q}_{(t+k)}^k$ converge towards limiting distributions, for any value of $k$.

Let us now consider $\mathbf{q}_t^t$. This set contains a single element: the sub-vector of those who have moved each time between time 0 and time $t$. This vector is $\mathbf{p}_0 [\mathbf{R}(0) - \mathbf{D}(0)]^t$. It converges towards 0 (assuming, as usual, that $\mathbf{R}(0)$ is entirely positive). In other words, we may assume that for large values of $t$

$$[\mathbf{R}(0) - \mathbf{D}(0)]^t \sim [\mathbf{R}(0) - \mathbf{D}(0)]^{(t-1)} \qquad (3.48)$$

Let us now consider the set $\mathbf{q}_{(t+1)}^t$ corresponding to those who have moved every time but once up to $(t + 1)$. It is readily shown, that if $\mathbf{q}_t^t$ converges, all the elements of $\mathbf{q}_{(t+1)}^t$ also converge. The argument is similar to the argument presented in eqn. (3.37) et seq. Generally, the elements of $\mathbf{q}_{(t+k)}^t$ will all converge, for any value of $k$.

Now, if the elements of $\mathbf{q}_{(t+k)}^t$ converge, the elements of $\mathbf{q}_{(t+k)}^0, \mathbf{q}_{(t+k)}^1, ..., \mathbf{q}_{(t+k)}^{(t-1)}$ also converge. In the same way, if the elements of $\mathbf{q}_{(t+k)}^t$ converge, the elements of $\mathbf{q}_{(t+k)}^{(t+1)}$, $\mathbf{q}_{(t+k)}^{(t+2)}, ..., \mathbf{q}_{(t+k)}^{(t+k)}$ also converge.

Now, we have supposed that for sufficiently large but finite values of $t$

$$\mathbf{D}(t) \sim \mathbf{D}(t-1) \qquad (3.49)$$

and

$$[\mathbf{R}(0) - \mathbf{D}(0)]^t \sim [\mathbf{R}(0) - \mathbf{D}(0)]^{(t-1)} \qquad (3.50)$$

Letting $k = t$, the above statements show that all the elements of the sets

$$\mathbf{q}_{2t}^0, \mathbf{q}_{2t}^1, \mathbf{q}_{2t}^2, ..., \mathbf{q}_{2t}^{2t}$$

converge towards a limiting distribution. Thus, if we observe the process at time $2t$ ($t$ finite), all the sub-vectors with sum equal to $\mathbf{p}_{2t}$, the overall distribution at time $2t$, converge towards a limiting distribution. In other words,

$$\mathbf{p}_{2t} \sim \mathbf{p}_{(2t-1)} \tag{3.51}$$

Much further work is needed, both on the theoretical behavior of the Cornell Model and on its possible empirical explorations. Let us only mention, in the conclusion of this presentation, that the Cornell Model should be considered as a family of models rather than as a single model. In the discussion of the axiomatics of this model, we have shown, that, besides the form of the cumulative inertia axiom considered by McGinnis himself (form A of the axiom), other forms are possible. In the preceding development, we used a distinct procedure (form B). But form C could also be used. Other procedures can also be devised. Thus, in the version of the model due to Henry and his coworkers, only a finite number of durations are considered. In this version, if someone has stayed in the same social position for, say, $k$ consecutive time units, his transition probabilities then are assumed to remain constant.

Finally, let us mention that Ginsberg (1971) has given a continuous version of the Cornell Model.

## 3.6. Pseudo-Markovian models with heterogeneous sub-populations

In this section, we shall consider another attempt to cope with the problem raised by underestimation of the amount of stability over time in job turnover generated by ordinary Markov chains. This attempt is due to McFarland (1970). His pseudo-Markovian model is represented in the tree of Fig. 3.1 by the lowest branch.

The contention of McFarland's model is that the empirical excess in the amount of stability for predictions derived from the Markov chains models may be explained by the heterogeneity of the population. In the models with individual or collective history as well as in the mover—stayer models, the explanation of the excess stability is, so to speak, tautological: all these models introduce, in one form or another, the assumption either that the overall trend towards stability increases, or that some sub-classes of people become increasingly stable as time elapses, or, alternatively, as in the mover—stayer models, that some individuals simply never move. All these assumptions, whatever their particular form, will obviously generate more stability than the predictions from a Markov chain.

McFarland's assumption is intellectually appealing because it explains the trend towards stability by a factor which has apparently no connection with stability, *i.e.* the heterogeneity of the population. It should, however, be noted that this assumption is not unrelated to the mover—stayer model. In this latter model, two latent classes are assumed, one defined by a diagonal and consequently unit transition matrix and called a class of stayers.

In McFarland's model, the number of classes is supposed to be *g* (eventually greater than 2). On the other hand, while each of these classes is characterized by a distinct transition matrix, none of these matrices is assumed necessarily to be the identity matrix. Finally, the transition matrices are assumed to be stationary, *i.e.* constant over time.

These assumptions may be used in three distinct ways.

(1) First, theoretically, the interesting question is whether a model of this kind actually generates a larger degree of stability than the corresponding Markov chain. This is the main question McFarland considers in his paper.

(2) Secondly, the assumptions suggest the definition of a model which could actually be applied to empirical data. Let us suppose we partition our population into *g* classes, using some observed variable as a partition criterion. Then, McFarland's assumptions yield a pseudo-Markovian model with one *observed* intervening variable. If this variable is age, we return to a simple version of the pseudo-cohort model with collective history dealt with in Section 3.4. Thus, if we substitute into eqn. (3.17) zero matrices for all the $X$ matrices and consequently identity matrices for all the $K$ matrices, we obtain a particular application of McFarland's model. But we may also use other kinds of intervening variables.

(3) Thirdly, they suggest the definition of a latent class mobility model. In this case, the variable according to which the population is partitioned is *latent* rather than observed. In other words we suppose that the population is a sum of sub-populations, characterized each by a different transition matrix. However, these sub-populations are not directly observable. Obviously, such a model is without solution if further assumptions are not introduced. The model presented in Section 2.5 may be useful in this respect: it suggests a partition of the overall population into sub-populations

96

which are characterized not only by distinct transition matrices, but also by distinct perfect mobility transition matrices. With this further assumption about the perfect mobility character of the latent transition matrices, we derive a version of McFarland's model which is simply an application of the model proposed by the present author in Section 2.5 to a sequence of matrices ordered in time rather than to a single matrix. This extension is straightforward: the turnover matrix corresponding to the first time interval may be analyzed exactly as described in Section 2.5 and in the statistical Appendix. Then, the sub-populations, as well as the latent transition matrices, are supposed constant over time, so that the parameters estimated from the first turnover matrix may be used to predict the distributions and gross turnover matrices for the following time intervals. Since the rationale for this latent model was extensively dealt with in Section 2.5, we shall not return to it, but simply stress that, when applied to a sequence of mobility matrices, it is an interesting member of the family of pseudo-Markovian models for heterogeneous populations.

In the same way, the rationale for the models referred to under (2) was dealt with in Section 3.4. Thus, we shall be content, in this section, to deal with point (1), which is the main point of McFarland's paper: to show that the assumption of heterogeneity of the population provides an alternative explanation of the trend towards stability observed in most empirical sets of data.

Thus, let us assume that a population may be divided in some way into $g$ classes, each characterized by a distinct and constant transition matrix. The matrix $\mathbf{R}_m$ will characterize the class $m$. Let, on the other hand, $\mathbf{D}_m = \text{diag } [d_{im}]$ be a diagonal matrix, where $d_{im}$ is the number of people belonging to class $m$, with initial status $i$ (the $g$ classes should not, of course, be confused with the social status categories which we shall suppose numbered from 1 to $\sigma$). Finally, let $\mathbf{D}^{-1} = \text{diag } [1/d_i]$ be also a diagonal matrix, the elements of which are the reciprocals of the total numbers of people initially located in each of the social status categories.

Then, the $t$-step transition matrix $\mathbf{R}^{(t)}$ for the total population will be

$$\mathbf{R}^{(t)} = \mathbf{D}^{-1} \sum_m \mathbf{D}_m \mathbf{R}_m{}^t \qquad (3.52)$$

A well-known theorem for Markov chains (see Section 2.2) states that, for each $m$, a matrix $\mathbf{R}_m{}^*$ exists such that

$$\lim_t \mathbf{R}_m{}^t = \mathbf{R}_m{}^* \qquad (3.53)$$

Whence, a matrix $\mathbf{R}^{(*)}$ also exists such that

$$\lim_t \mathbf{R}^{(t)} = \mathbf{R}^{(*)} \qquad (3.54)$$

But this limiting matrix need not be the same as the corresponding Markov chain matrix.

Let us now see how the model (3.52) provides an alternative explanation of the excess stability phenomenon. On this point we shall content ourself with quoting McFarland: "The expected proportion of persons in a given status who make any particular transition is equal by eqn. (3.52), to the average of their various probabilities of doing so. Now, those who leave the given status during the first time interval differ from those who remain, in that the latter tend to be persons with higher probabilities of staying than the former. Thus, the group remaining after one time period will have a higher average probability of staying than did the initial group; and hence the expected proportion of the former group remaining throughout the second time period is larger than the expected proportion of the initial group remaining throughout the first time period."

Let us suppose $g=2$, for the sake of illustration, and consider the following fictitious matrices.

$$\mathbf{D}_1 = \begin{bmatrix} 10 & 0 \\ 0 & 40 \end{bmatrix} \qquad \mathbf{D}_2 = \begin{bmatrix} 40 & 0 \\ 0 & 10 \end{bmatrix}$$

$$\mathbf{R}_1 = \begin{bmatrix} 0.6 & 0.4 \\ 0.4 & 0.6 \end{bmatrix} \qquad \mathbf{R}_2 = \begin{bmatrix} 0.5 & 0.5 \\ 0.5 & 0.5 \end{bmatrix}$$

It is readily verified, using eqn. (3.52), that $\mathbf{R}^{(2)}$ does not have larger diagonal elements than $\mathbf{R}^{(1)}$. Indeed

$$\mathbf{R}^{(1)} = \begin{bmatrix} 0.520 & 0.480 \\ 0.480 & 0.520 \end{bmatrix} \qquad \mathbf{R}^{(2)} = \begin{bmatrix} 0.504 & 0.496 \\ 0.484 & 0.516 \end{bmatrix}$$

However, $\mathbf{R}^{(2)}$ has larger diagonal elements than $[\mathbf{R}^{(1)}]^2$, *i.e.* the transition matrix from initial time to time 2 which we obtain under the assumption of a Markov chain

$$[\mathbf{R}^{(1)}]^2 = \begin{bmatrix} 0.501 & 0.499 \\ 0.499 & 0.501 \end{bmatrix}$$

McFarland's idea of explaining the excess stability by the heterogeneity of the population is important, not only because it gives an original interpretation of this phenomenon, but also because it advances a step in the direction of sociological realism. Girod (1971) and Blau and Duncan (1967), as well as many mobility students, have shown that the moves of an individual depend not only on his current status or on the history of his moves, but also on other variables such as his social origin. McFarland's model could include this empirical statement, since this latter variable can be used to partition an original population into a set of subpopulations with distinct social origins.

More generally, this model is an important step towards solving a previously mentioned dilemma: the mathematical methods used in social mobility studies are usually either general statistical methods (such as causal analysis) which may include as many intervening variables as desired but are syntactically poor, or more sophisticated instruments which include no or few intervening variables. McFarland's model indicates how a synthesis between the two approaches may eventually be reached.

## 3.7. Job mobility instead of individual mobility

White's (1970a) vacancy model is particularly worth mentioning in this presentation of the main trends of research in intragenerational mobility. It represents not only a new model, but also a new approach to the "system models of mobility in organizations", as the subtitle of White's book states. The important difference between the previous intragenerational model and White's model is that, in this latter model, the mobility of the individuals is explicitly treated as a dependent variable: the appearance of vacancies in a system of jobs comes first in the causal ordering. When new vacancies have been created, they give rise to further vacancies which in their turn are filled, etc. Thus, the mobility of the men is treated as the mirror image of the mobility of the vacancies.

This approach is of particular relevance in the analysis of mobility within organizations. Here, beyond doubt, the initiative belongs actually with the vacancies rather than with the men. Thus, the importance of White's work appears immediately as far as microsociological intragenerational mobility is concerned. But it suggests also a new approach in macrosociological mobility research. It would be hazardous to say that a social system as a whole should be considered as a huge organization. But such a system may be considered as a set of organizations. Whether the vacancy model can be applied in this broader case is a question which can only be answered by further research and applications. However, it offers an original approach, the applicability of which, to macrosociological research, is worth investigation. Its basic statement that mobility should be made dependent on the social structure is certainly a step towards the reconciliation of the mathematical theory of mobility with the sociological theory.

*The rationale for the vacancy model*

It is, of course, impossible to present the vacancy model fully. We shall be content with a brief presentation of the model in its simplest version. Then, we shall report some of the consequences of the model for the turnover of individuals.

Let us consider a set of jobs partitioned into $\sigma$ strata and call $q_{ij}$ the probability that a vacancy moves from stratum $i$ to stratum $j$. Further, suppose that any vacancy must leave the system after some fixed maximum span of time and call $q_{i0}$ the probability of a vacancy going from stratum $i$ out of the system. Then

$$\sum_{j=0} q_{ij} = 1 \tag{3.55}$$

Let us call **Q** the matrix $[q_{ij}]$ with $i, j = 1$ to $\sigma$, **q** the column vector $q_{i0}$, and **u** a conformable unit column vector. Then

$$\mathbf{Qu} + \mathbf{q} = \mathbf{u} \tag{3.56}$$

Now consider the probability that a vacancy starting in stratum $i$ remains in the system during $t$ time units and call this probability $s_{it}$. With the assumption that the vacancies move according to a Markov chain, the column vector $\mathbf{s}_t = [s_{it}]$ is related to **Q** and **q** by

$$\mathbf{s}_t = \mathbf{Q}^{(t-1)}\mathbf{q} \tag{3.57}$$

Let $\mathbf{v} = [v_i]$ be the column vector describing the average span of time during which a vacancy starting in stratum $i$ remains in the system. Then, from eqn. (3.56)

$$q = (I - Q)u \qquad (3.58)$$

and, from eqns. (3.57) and (3.58)

$$v = \sum_t ts_t$$

$$= \sum_t tQ^{(t-1)}q$$

$$= (I-Q)^{-2}q$$

$$= (I-Q)^{-1}u \qquad (3.59)$$

The next step is to consider a set of vacancies arriving in the system at the initial time. Let $f = [f_i]$ be a row vector describing the number of vacancies arriving in each stratum and $p = [p_i]$ be a row vector describing the proportions of vacancies arriving in each stratum at the initial time. Then

$$fs_t = fQ^{(t-1)}q \qquad (3.60)$$

is the number of vacancies which remain in the system during $t$ time units and

$$pv = p \sum_t ts_t = p(I-Q)^{-1}u \qquad (3.61)$$

the average time a vacancy stays in the system.

We come now to a crucial relationship in White's vacancy model. The problem is to derive the number $m_i$ of moves made from stratum $i$ by a set of vacancies and the total number

$$M = \sum_i m_i \qquad (3.62)$$

of these moves. Let us call $m$ the row vector $[m_i]$.

To solve this problem, we first note that $f$ is the count of first moves by stratum. Indeed, let us, for instance, consider $f_i$, the number of vacancies arriving in stratum $i$. Since the vacancies will move at the next step (some of them moving from $i$ to $i$), $f_i$ is the number of vacancies which will leave $i$ during the first move. In the same way, the $i$th element of $fQ$ is the number of vacancies which arrive in stratum $i$ at the end of the first move, or, alternatively, the number of vacancies which start from $i$ for the next move.

101

Thus

$$\mathbf{m} = \sum_{t=0} \mathbf{f} \mathbf{Q}^t = \mathbf{f} (\mathbf{I} - \mathbf{Q})^{-1} \tag{3.63}$$

where, by convention, $\mathbf{Q}^0 = \mathbf{I}$, the identity matrix. The total number of vacancies which ever moved from any stratum is

$$M = \mathbf{mu} = \mathbf{f}(\mathbf{I} - \mathbf{Q})^{-1}\mathbf{u} = \mathbf{fv} \tag{3.64}$$

*Some applications*

The model can be applied to predict the distribution of the vacancy chain lengths. Indeed, when $\mathbf{Q}$ has been estimated from some data, eqn. (3.57) may be used to predict the probability that a vacancy starting in stratum $i$ will leave the system after $t$ time units. In the empirical illustration of his model, White uses data dealing with a church organization. For occupational strata he uses, as a criterion, the number of communicants attached to pastoral jobs and groups these numbers into broad classes. Then he uses a sophisticated coding of the recorded pastoral moves in order to obtain an estimate for f and $\mathbf{Q}$. The general agreement between the predicted and the observed chain lengths is good.

Since detailed presentation of the applications of this model is beyond the scope of this book, we shall concentrate on the consequences of the model for the turnover of individuals. This has the advantage of allowing for a comparison with the previous intragenerational models. We shall closely follow White in this exposition.

Let us suppose the process described by the previous equations goes on, say, for one year. On the other hand, let us assume that during this time, the individuals are allowed to move just once. (This time unit should not be confounded with the abstract time unit $t$ referred to above, which describes the steps of a vacancy chain, so that many of these units are included in one year.) Allowing the individuals to move just once in one year parallels the assumption of the usual intragenerational models defined for individuals: in all these models, the individuals are allowed to move just once in the time unit (a quarter in Blumen's model, a year elsewhere).

Let us now consider eqn. (3.63) which gives, as we recall, the total number of vacancies starting from the various social strata, and suppose a vacancy moves from $j$ to $i$. This means that one man has moved from $i$ to $j$. Now, the total number of vacancies starting from $j$ is $m_j$ and the probability of a vacancy moving from $j$ to $i$ is $q_{ji}$. Thus $m_j q_{ji}$ is the total number of vacancies that move from $j$ to $i$. If we suppose a man can only move once a year, this latter quantity is also the number of people moving from $i$ to $j$. Let us call this number

$$n_{ij} = m_j q_{ji} \qquad (i \neq j) \tag{3.65}$$

Suppose $i = j$. This means that we are considering the vacancies starting in stratum $i$ and going to $i$. Some of these moves correspond to moves of men within $i$. But others result from the fact that some people enter and leave the system.

Let us now consider two consecutive years $y$ and $(y + 1)$ and apply eqn. (3.65).

$$n_{ij}(y) = m_j(y)q_{ji}(y) \tag{3.66a}$$

$$n_{ij}(y + 1) = m_j(y + 1)q_{ji}(y + 1) \tag{3.66b}$$

If we also assume that $\mathbf{Q}$ is the same from one year to the next, eqn. (3.66) yields

$$\frac{n_{ij}(y + 1)}{n_{ij}(y)} = \frac{m_j(y + 1)}{m_j(y)} \tag{3.67}$$

For a Markov chain model defined directly on the individuals, we have, by contrast

$$n_{ij}(y) = n_i(y)r_{ij}(y) \tag{3.68a}$$

$$n_{ij}(y + 1) = n_i(y + 1)r_{ij}(y + 1) \tag{3.68b}$$

where $n_i$ is the number of people coming from $i$ and $r_{ij}$ the transition probability for an individual coming from $i$ and going to $j$.

As a consequence of the stationarity assumption, eqn. (3.68) yields

$$\frac{n_{ij}(y + 1)}{n_{ij}(y)} = \frac{n_i(y + 1)}{n_i(y)} \tag{3.69}$$

This very simple result suggests, as White points out, a simple test which is useful for deciding between the individual Markov chain model and the vacancy model for a given set of data. If the former applies, the ratios $n_{ij}(y+1)/n_{ij}(y)$ should be constant for all values of $j$, given $i$. If the latter applies, the same ratios should be constant for all values of $i$, given $j$. This shows that even with parallel assumptions (one move during each time unit, stationarity), the vacancy Markov chain model leads to predictions for the turnover of the individuals which are distinct from those which derive from the usual individual Markov chain model.

White has also analyzed the form taken by $R^{(y)}$, the overall transition matrix of the individuals between time 0 and time $y$. He has shown that even with Markovian assumptions (one move during each time unit, stationarity), the vacancy model does not lead to $R^{(y)} = R^y$, in contrast to the Markov chain model defined on the individuals which does. But this latter result derives less from the vacancy-rather-than-men approach than from the death assumption included in the model. This assumption makes the vacancy model logically very different from the usual intragenerational mobility models. Here, it is generally not assumed that men leave the system, while in the vacancy model, vacancies do leave. We shall, however, meet this death process in some intergenerational mobility models of the last chapter.

In conclusion, the vacancy model is certainly a promising tool for the study of mobility within organizations, although its Markov chain assumptions must certainly be refined in order to make the model applicable to certain situations (vacancies, like men, may, for instance, sometimes move as a function of their "individual history"). Its application to other social frameworks is a matter for further investigation.

CHAPTER 4

# Theories Using Intervening Variables

## 4.1. Introduction

In the previous chapters, we considered models including, for the most part, no explicit intervening variables. These models were of two kinds: in some cases, no intervening variables, either implicit or explicit were introduced; but in most cases implicit intervening variables were present as in White's intergenerational model. In this latter case, while the data are restricted to the usual mobility tables, they are interpreted with the help of unobservable variables, such as the distinction stayers/movers. On the other hand, some models, such as the Cornell Mobility Model use observed intervening variables (duration of stay in one state). But these variables are built from mobility matrices without using any additional outside information. These models with unobserved intervening variables or with observed intervening variables built from mobility matrices are adequate particularly in the field of intragenerational mobility. Here, several successive turnover matrices are available, so that estimation procedures may be derived for the parameters, using, for instance, as in the case of Blumen's model, the equilibrium distribution. On the other hand, the time unit for intragenerational mobility, is often short so that it may not be too unrealistic to assume stability of the structural factors which are, at least partly, responsible for the amount of observed mobility.

When dealing with intergenerational mobility, the situation is clearly different. It is much more difficult in this case to use sophisticated models including unobserved intervening variables, since the data will generally not allow estimation of the latent

105

parameters. In particular, the interpretation of the equilibrium distribution may be questionable. On the other hand, given the length of the time unit it may become unrealistic in the intergenerational case to ignore the structural changes which may affect the mobility processes.

This does not imply that models with unobserved intervening variables are inapplicable when dealing with intergenerational mobility. Goodman's models and White's intergenerational mover—stayer model of Section 3.4 as well as the generalized version of these models analyzed in Section 3.5 show that this type of model may be useful in the intergenerational case. The previous remarks suggest, however, that an alternative strategy certainly to be taken into account is to introduce relevant explicit intervening variables. Differential fertility is undoubtedly one of these variables which influence the mobility processes. To our knowledge, this variable was first explicitly introduced by Kahl (1957) in his classical work on social mobility. Later, Matras (1961) formalized Kahl's idea and proposed a model in which differential fertility was introduced as an intervening variable in the mobility process. But many other relevant intervening variables, of course, exist, such as variables related to the educational system. These variables are currently used in mobility studies using statistical methods, and, more rarely, in mathematical mobility models. Thus, in their study on social stratification in America, Blau and Duncan (1967) use individual intervening variables such as the father's and the respondent's levels of education. In this respect, the use of mathematical rather than of statistical language has the advantage of clarifying the relationships between the structural variables (*e.g.* changes in the educational and/or social structure) and the individual variables currently used in empirical social mobility research. We shall return to this crucial point later.

*Types of models*

The intergenerational mobility models with explicit intervening variables may be classified according to several taxonomic dimensions.

(1) A number of these models treat the variables characterizing the social structures and their changes as independent variables, while social mobility is considered as the dependent variable. In models of this type, the differential fertility or the changes in the occupational structures are, for instance, taken as independent

106

variables explaining (at least partially) the mobility between two successive generations. A second class of models (which appeared first, historically) takes social mobility as the independent and the changes in the social structure as the dependent variable. In this case, assumptions are made about the structure of the mobility process whence statements are derived about the resulting changes in the social structure.

This latter approach may be found for instance, in the Prais model already studied (Section 2.2). Some authors, such as Matras in some of his work, have used a similar approach, but have introduced intervening variables, such as differential fertility, into the relationship between social structure and social mobility.

This approach may, of course, appear as contradicting basic sociological axioms. For a sociologist, the assumption that the structure of the mobility processes may cause changes in the social structures is quite unrealistic. It seems much more realistic to assume the reverse causal ordering. Perhaps this type of model was unconsciously generated by the first attempts to apply Markov chain models to social mobility, since the transition matrices used in these models have precisely the effect of transforming a social structure observed at time $t$ into another social structure at time $(t+1)$.

In spite of these objections, we shall present here some models in which the social mobility structure is taken as the independent variable, since some of these models provide important steps towards a formal theory of social mobility.

(2) A second possible classification involves the number of intervening variables introduced. Sometimes, differential fertility alone, or differential fertility plus changes in the occupational structure are, for instance, used to predict the mobility processes. In other cases, different variables are introduced, *e.g.* variables pertaining to the educational system. This classification is certainly important, since a realistic model should certainly include all the intervening variables which influence significantly the mobility processes.

(3) A third major classification deals with the kind of formal instruments used. Generally, two main kinds of tools may be distinguished: general statistical methods (such as path analysis) and mathematical process analysis. As already mentioned, classifications (2) and (3) are obviously related. This connection derives from the fact that it is much easier to introduce many intervening variables into, say, a multiple regression model with several equa-

107

tions than into a stochastic model. Again, a basic strategy is to attempt to increase the number of relevant intervening variables in stochastic mobility models.

*Overview of the chapter*

In Section 4.2, we shall discuss the model derived by Matras (1961) from Kahl's (1957) work. In this model, social mobility is treated as an independent variable. In Section 4.3, we shall present a model proposed by the present author, in which social mobility is taken as a dependent variable resulting from the combined effects of a number of independent and intervening variables (differential fertility, changes in the educational and occupational structures, inequality of educational opportunities, etc.). In Section 4.3, this model will be presented in its generational and pseudo-cohort versions. The presentation of its true cohort version will be delayed until the end of Section 4.4. In the first two subsections of Section 4.4, we shall present a basic model, again originally proposed by Matras. This model is potentially a very useful tool for the analysis of social mobility. Matras (1966) mentions that it was suggested to him by a demographic model due to Keyfitz (1964). Later, Coleman (1971) provided an interesting adaptation of this model, which allows it to be applied to educational mobility data. Thus, we shall present both Matras' original formulation of the model and Coleman's reformulation. Finally, in the last sub-section of Section 4.4, we shall propose a synthesis of the Matras cohort model with the model proposed by the present author in Section 4.3. This yields a true cohort model in which social mobility is conceived as a dependent variable influenced by a set of independent intervening variables.

## 4.2. A model including differential fertility as an intervening variable and treating social mobility as an independent variable

As mentioned above, the first model we are going to analyze was inspired by Kahl's (1957) work. It makes social mobility an independent and social structure a dependent variable. Although this causal ordering is questionable, the Matras model is worth considering, since it represents the first attempt to analyze the relationship between social mobility and differential fertility.

108

*The rationale for the model*

Let $\mathbf{R} = [r_{ij}]$, as usual, be the transition matrix describing the probabilities for a family coming from $i$ and going to $j$. Let, on the other hand, $\mathbf{p}_0 = [p_{(0)i}]$ be a row vector describing the proportion of families belonging to the occupational categories $1, 2, ..., i, ..., \sigma$ at time 0. Finally, let $\mathbf{D} = \text{diag}[d_i]$ be a diagonal matrix describing the ratio of the net reproduction rate of the $i$th social category to the reproduction rate of the whole population. Then, if $f$ is the overall reproduction rate, the $i$th element of $\mathbf{D}$ will be $f_i/f$, where $f_i$ is the reproduction rate of the $i$th class.

Now, call $\mathbf{q}_1$ the distribution according to social origin of the sons with fathers distributed according to $\mathbf{p}_0$. Then

$$\mathbf{p}_0 \mathbf{D} = \mathbf{q}_1 \qquad (4.1)$$

Again, $\mathbf{p}_0$ describes the distribution of the fathers according to their socio-occupational classification, while $\mathbf{q}_1$ describes the distribution of these fathers' sons according to social origin. Then, these sons will attain a social status of their own, as generated by the transition matrix $\mathbf{R}$. Call $\mathbf{p}_1$ the distribution of the sons in the various social categories, after they have their own status. Then

$$\mathbf{q}_1 \mathbf{R} = \mathbf{p}_1 \qquad (4.2)$$

Or, substituting eqn. (4.1) into eqn. (4.2)

$$\mathbf{q}_1 \mathbf{R} = \mathbf{p}_0 \mathbf{D} \mathbf{R} = \mathbf{p}_1 \qquad (4.3)$$

Now, it must be realized that this notation, which is correct if we consider two generations, has to be modified by the introduction of a time index when more generations are considered. Indeed, let us suppose we want to extend the process (4.3) to the following generation. Then, we should first have to generate a vector $\mathbf{q}_2 = [q_{(2)i}]$ describing the distribution according to social origin of the sons whose fathers are described by $\mathbf{p}_1$. But we cannot generate this vector simply by postmultiplying $\mathbf{p}_1$ by $\mathbf{D}$, since we cannot assume that $\mathbf{p}_1 \mathbf{D}$ will be a vector with elements summing to 1. In other words, assume that $\mathbf{p}_1 \neq \mathbf{p}_0$ and suppose the differential fertility rate to be constant over time. Then, $f$, the overall reproduction rate will vary with time and should rather be denoted by $f(t)$. As a consequence, $\mathbf{D} = \text{diag}[d_i] = \text{diag}[f_i/f]$ should be denoted by $\mathbf{D}_t$. Then, we rewrite eqns. (4.1) $-$ (4.3) in the following way.

$$\mathbf{p}_0\mathbf{D}_0 = \mathbf{q}_1 \tag{4.4}$$

$$\mathbf{q}_1\mathbf{R} = \mathbf{p}_0\mathbf{D}_0\mathbf{R} = \mathbf{p}_1 \tag{4.5}$$

We can now extend the process to the following generation.

$$\mathbf{p}_1\mathbf{D}_1 = \mathbf{q}_2 \tag{4.6}$$

$$\mathbf{q}_2\mathbf{R} = \mathbf{p}_1\mathbf{D}_1\mathbf{R} = \mathbf{p}_2 \tag{4.7}$$

or, substituting eqn. (4.5) into eqn. (4.7)

$$\mathbf{p}_1\mathbf{D}_1\mathbf{R} = \mathbf{p}_0\mathbf{D}_0\mathbf{R}\mathbf{D}_1\mathbf{R} = \mathbf{p}_2 \tag{4.8}$$

Extending the process to the $t$th generation, it is readily shown that

$$\mathbf{p}_0\mathbf{D}_0\mathbf{R}\mathbf{D}_1\mathbf{R}\mathbf{D}_2\mathbf{R} \dots \mathbf{D}_{(t-1)}\mathbf{R} = \mathbf{p}_t \tag{4.9}$$

If we assume

$$\mathbf{D}_0 = \mathbf{I} \tag{4.10}$$

where $\mathbf{I}$ is the identity matrix, all fertility rates are equal: the fertility of all social classes is the same. In this case

$$\mathbf{D}_0 = \mathbf{D}_1 = \dots = \mathbf{D}_{(t-1)} = \mathbf{I} \tag{4.11}$$

Then, eqn. (4.9) reduces to

$$\mathbf{p}_0\mathbf{R}^t = \mathbf{p}_t \tag{4.12}$$

Thus, with no differences in fertility rates, the model generates an ordinary Markov chain of the type described in Section 2.2.

If differences are assumed in the fertility rate according to social class, we return to eqn. (4.9), a model with much more complicated behavior.

*Introducing the assumption of perfect mobility*

As Bartholomew (1967) has pointed out, the behavior of this model is easily analyzed if we introduce the supplementary assumption that $\mathbf{R}$ is a perfect mobility matrix. Then, by the definition of perfect mobility which makes the achieved status independent of the origin status, $\mathbf{R}$ will be a matrix with all rows the same. Otherwise, the destination status would depend on the origin status.

Now, it is readily verified that, if $\mathbf{R}$ is a matrix with all rows the same

$$\mathbf{p}_1 = \mathbf{p}_0 \mathbf{D}_0 \mathbf{R} \tag{4.13}$$

is a row vector identical to the rows of $\mathbf{R}$. In the same way

$$\mathbf{p}_2 = \mathbf{p}_1 \mathbf{D}_1 \mathbf{R} \tag{4.14}$$

and, generally,

$$\mathbf{p}_t = \mathbf{p}_{(t-1)} \mathbf{D}_{(t-1)} \mathbf{R} \tag{4.15}$$

will be row vectors identical to the rows of $\mathbf{R}$. Then, we have

$$\mathbf{p}_1 = \mathbf{p}_2 = \ldots = \mathbf{p}_{(t-1)} = \mathbf{p}_t = \text{etc.} \tag{4.16}$$

all these vectors being equal to the rows of $\mathbf{R}$ which are themselves all equal.

In summary: when $\mathbf{R}$ is a perfect mobility matrix, the differential fertility factor has no effect. The social structure (*i.e.* the distribution of the individuals in the various socio-occupational categories) remains stable over time.

*Dropping the assumption of perfect mobility*

When perfect mobility is not assumed, the differential fertility factor has an effect on the social structure.

For complete immobility, *i.e.* when $\mathbf{R} = \mathbf{I}$, the identity matrix, eqn. (4.9) becomes

$$\mathbf{p}_0 \mathbf{D}_0 \mathbf{D}_1 \mathbf{D}_2 \ldots \mathbf{D}_{(t-1)} = \mathbf{p}_t \tag{4.17}$$

Then, the whole population will, in the limit, be located in the social class having the greatest fertility rate if, of course, there is such a class.

In the intermediary cases, *i.e.* when $\mathbf{R}$ is neither a perfect mobility matrix, nor a unit matrix, the behavior of the model is more complicated. However, it can still be shown that the process converges towards a limiting distribution.

Let us call $\mathbf{F}$ a diagonal matrix

$$\mathbf{F} = \text{diag}\,[f_i] \tag{4.18}$$

describing the reproduction rates. Then, let us substitute the vectors $\mathbf{n}_0$, $\mathbf{n}_1$, etc. for $\mathbf{p}_0$, $\mathbf{p}_1$, etc. in eqn. (4.1) et seq. with, as usual,

111

$$\mathbf{n}_0 = [n_{(0)i}] \tag{4.19a}$$

$$\mathbf{n}_1 = [n_{(1)i}] \tag{4.19b}$$

$n_{(0)i}$ being the *number* of people belonging to social category $i$ at generation 0, $n_{(1)i}$ the number belonging to $i$ at generation 1, etc. Then, eqn. (4.20) may be substituted for eqn. (4.1)

$$\mathbf{n}_0 \mathbf{F} = \mathbf{m}_1 \tag{4.20}$$

The vector $\mathbf{m}_1 = [m_{(1)i}]$ gives the number of sons with social origins 1, 2, ..., $i$, ..., $\sigma$, while

$$\mathbf{m}_1 \mathbf{R} = \mathbf{n}_1 \tag{4.21}$$

gives the number of sons belonging to social categories 1, 2, ..., $i$, ..., $\sigma$, once they are adults. Substituting eqn. (4.20) into eqn. (4.21), we obtain

$$\mathbf{n}_0 \mathbf{FR} = \mathbf{n}_1 \tag{4.22}$$

Using numbers rather than proportions has the effect that $\mathbf{F}$, by contrast to $\mathbf{D}$, need not be time indexed. Thus, the distribution at the $t$th generation is related to the distribution at generation 0 by

$$\mathbf{n}_0 (\mathbf{FR})^t = \mathbf{n}_t \tag{4.23}$$

Let us now consider the limiting behavior of $(\mathbf{FR})^t$. $\mathbf{FR}$ is obviously not a matrix with row sums all equal to 1 *. However, let us assume that the largest row sum of $\mathbf{FR}$ is smaller than or equal to some number $a$ and call $\mathbf{A}^{-1}$ the scalar matrix diag$[1/a]$. Then, all the row sums of $\mathbf{A}^{-1}\mathbf{FR}$ are $\leqslant 1$.

Let us now border $\mathbf{A}^{-1}\mathbf{FR}$ by a row

$$\mathbf{r}_{0j} = [\underbrace{1\ 0\ 0\ ...\ 0\ ...\ 0}_{\sigma + 1 \text{ elements}}] \tag{4.24a}$$

and by a column

---

* See Feller (1950), pp. 374–375

$$\mathbf{r}_{i0} = \begin{bmatrix} 1 \\ d_1 \\ d_2 \\ \vdots \\ d_i \\ \vdots \\ d_\sigma \end{bmatrix} \quad , \tag{4.24b}$$

where $d_i$ is the (positive) difference between 1 and the $i$th row total of $\mathbf{A}^{-1}\mathbf{FR}$. Let us call $\mathbf{Q}$ the resulting matrix. $\mathbf{Q}$ is a matrix with all row sums equal to 1 and all elements $\geqslant 0$ and $\leqslant 1$. Thus, $\mathbf{Q}^t$ converges towards a limit. For large $t$

$$\mathbf{Q}^{(t+1)} \sim \mathbf{Q}^t \tag{4.25}$$

Now, $(\mathbf{A}^{-1}\mathbf{FR})^t$ is a sub-matrix of $\mathbf{Q}^t$. This shows that, for large $t$

$$(\mathbf{A}^{-1}\mathbf{FR})^{(t+1)} \sim (\mathbf{A}^{-1}\mathbf{FR})^t \tag{4.26}$$

Finally, since $\mathbf{A}$ is a scalar matrix, we may write eqn. (4.23) in the following way

$$\mathbf{n}_0(\mathbf{FR})^t = \mathbf{n}_0\mathbf{A}^t(\mathbf{A}^{-1}\mathbf{FR})^t = \mathbf{n}_t \tag{4.27a}$$

extend this equation to the next generation

$$\mathbf{n}_0(\mathbf{FR})^{(t+1)} = \mathbf{n}_0\mathbf{A}^{(t+1)}(\mathbf{A}^{-1}\mathbf{FR})^{(t+1)} = \mathbf{n}_{(t+1)} \tag{4.27b}$$

and draw from eqn. (4.27)*

$$\mathbf{n}_{(t+1)} \sim \mathbf{n}_t\mathbf{A} \tag{4.28}$$

Or

$$\mathbf{P}_{(t+1)} \sim \mathbf{P}_t \tag{4.29}$$

since $\mathbf{A}$ is a scalar matrix.

Thus differential fertility does not destroy the convergence to-wards a limiting distribution.

---

*Obviously, although $(\mathbf{A}^{-1}\mathbf{FR})^t$ converges to 0 if all $d$'s are positive, $\mathbf{A}^t(\mathbf{A}^{-1}\mathbf{FR})^t$ does not, otherwise, by eqn. (4.27), the population would dis-appear in the limit even with an average fertility greater than 1.

Let us consider, for the sake of illustration, a numerical example. We shall assume the following parameters and initial conditions.

$$\mathbf{p}_0 = [0.6 \quad 0.4]$$

$$f_1 = 2, \quad f_2 = 1$$

$$\mathbf{R} = \begin{bmatrix} 0.6 & 0.4 \\ 0.2 & 0.8 \end{bmatrix}$$

These parameters generate the following sequence of distributions

$$\mathbf{p}_1 = \mathbf{p}_0 \mathbf{D}_0 \mathbf{R} = [0.6 \quad 0.4] \begin{bmatrix} 20/16 & 0 \\ 0 & 10/16 \end{bmatrix} \begin{bmatrix} 0.6 & 0.4 \\ 0.2 & 0.8 \end{bmatrix}$$

$$= [0.75 \quad 0.25] \begin{bmatrix} 0.6 & 0.4 \\ 0.2 & 0.8 \end{bmatrix} = [0.5 \quad 0.5]$$

$$\mathbf{p}_2 = \mathbf{p}_1 \mathbf{D}_1 \mathbf{R} = [0.5 \quad 0.5] \begin{bmatrix} 20/15 & 0 \\ 0 & 10/15 \end{bmatrix} \begin{bmatrix} 0.6 & 0.4 \\ 0.2 & 0.8 \end{bmatrix}$$

$$= [0.67 \quad 0.33] \begin{bmatrix} 0.6 & 0.4 \\ 0.2 & 0.8 \end{bmatrix} = [0.47 \quad 0.53]$$

$$\mathbf{p}_3 = \mathbf{p}_2 \mathbf{D}_2 \mathbf{R} = [0.47 \quad 0.53] \begin{bmatrix} 200/147 & 0 \\ 0 & 100/147 \end{bmatrix} \begin{bmatrix} 0.6 & 0.4 \\ 0.2 & 0.8 \end{bmatrix}$$

$$= [0.64 \quad 0.36] \begin{bmatrix} 0.6 & 0.4 \\ 0.2 & 0.8 \end{bmatrix} = [0.456 \quad 0.544]$$

$$\mathbf{p}_4 = \mathbf{p}_3 \mathbf{D}_3 \mathbf{R} = [0.456 \quad 0.544] \begin{bmatrix} 2000/1456 & 0 \\ 0 & 1000/1456 \end{bmatrix} \begin{bmatrix} 0.6 & 0.4 \\ 0.2 & 0.8 \end{bmatrix}$$

$$= [0.626 \quad 0.374] \begin{bmatrix} 0.6 & 0.4 \\ 0.2 & 0.8 \end{bmatrix} = [0.4504 \quad 0.5496]$$

etc.*.

----------

*As pointed out to me by Neil Henry, the equilibrium distribution $\mathbf{p}^*$ is the eigenvector corresponding to the largest eigenvalue of $\mathbf{FR}$ so that the exact result is $\mathbf{p}^* = [\sqrt{0.2}, 1-\sqrt{0.2}]$.

In this exploration, we have supposed that class 1 was both more fertile and more numerous at the initial time. If it was more fertile and less numerous, it is readily verified that $p_{(t)1}$ would still converge to a limiting value.

It is also interesting to note that the equilibrium distribution is affected by the assumption of differential fertility. Thus the parameters of the numerical illustration generate the equilibrium distribution (to two decimals)

$$\lim_t \mathbf{p}_t = [0.45 \quad 0.55] \tag{4.30}$$

Keeping the same values for $\mathbf{p}_0$ and $\mathbf{R}$ but setting

$$f_1 = f_2 \tag{4.31}$$

generates an ordinary Markov chain with equilibrium distribution

$$\lim_t \mathbf{p}_t = [0.33 \quad 0.67] \tag{4.32}$$

This suggests the intuitively expected result that differential fertility increases the relative size of the more fertile classes. On the other hand, the existence of a limiting distribution shows that differential fertility has an effect on the social structures only in the case where an equilibrium has not yet been reached. This result is less obvious and has an interesting social bearing, since it shows that the existence of differential fertility rates is not incompatible with stability of the social structure, even in the case where the transition matrix is stationary with complete immobility identity nor perfect mobility.

Another point is worth mentioning: if we compare eqns. (4.30) and (4.32) with the initial distribution $\mathbf{p}_0$, we see that the equilibrium distribution is closer to the initial distribution when the differential fertility assumption is introduced. While this result has, of course, no general bearing, it does show that, in some cases, an empirical distribution may be closer to equilibrium than if the assumption of differential fertility were not introduced.

Needless to say, the previous exploration of the dichotomous case is not a substitute for a formal analysis of the behavior of the model. But it may be sufficient to evaluate its potential usefulness for both theory and research. From the theoretical viewpoint, it shows that differential fertility may have, under given conditions, no effect on the social structures, not only when mobility is perfect, but also when it is imperfect. In other words, the stability of the social structures and of the mobility patterns is not necessarily incompatible with the existence of differential fertility rates.

Empirically, the Matras model was an important step towards realistic mathematical mobility models. Historically, in the attempts to formalize the mobility processes, it was certainly one of the first models to stress the necessity of introducing relevant intervening variables. The main weakness is, however, the causal ordering implicitly introduced between social mobility and social structure.

### 4.3. A model introducing several intervening variables where social mobility is treated as a dependent variable

We shall now discuss a model originally presented by the present author (1970, 1971a) in which mobility is treated as a dependent variable, while several independent intervening variables are simultaneously introduced. In this section, we shall present a generational and a pseudo-cohort version of the model. The exposition of the true cohort version will be delayed until Section 4.4.

Originally, this model derived from the difficulties met in interpreting some sets of empirical data concerning the relationship between education and mobility. Without going into detail, we shall mention briefly some intriguing results.

In a well-known paper, Anderson (1961) has shown that the correlation between education and socio-educational status may not be very high, even in the most advanced industrial societies. From a study by Centers on the U.S., Anderson drew a cross-tabulation between the relative educational status and the relative occupational status of a sample of sons as compared to that of their fathers. The table is much closer to a theoretical table constructed using the assumption of statistical independence between the variables (relative educational, relative occupational status) than to a table using the assumption of maximum effect of the educational on the occupational level. Data drawn from a Swedish and from a British survey led Anderson to the same conclusion: in all cases the relationship between education and mobility or between education and occupational status was much smaller than one would have intuitively expected in technologically and economically advanced societies.

Another study, led by the OECD (1970), also leads to puzzling results. This study uses the comparison of educational and occupa-

116

tional data in a large number of countries with different levels of development. The comparison shows that the greater the development of the educational system, the weaker the relationship at the individual level between educational and occupational status, at least when the highest educational levels are considered. Since the development of the educational system is correlated with general development, this shows that in the technologically and economically more advanced societies, the correlation between occupational and educational status can be lower than in less advanced societies*.

It is, of course, impossible to introduce here a detailed discussion of these results and of many others which could be referred to when dealing with this problem of the relationship between education and mobility. We shall restrict ourself to the general methodological conclusions which may be drawn from these studies. First, educational variables are certainly crucial in predicting the mobility processes. Secondly, the relationship between education and mobility is complex, including many factors: obviously, the technologically more advanced societies require better educated people. But, the relationship between education and occupational status may be lower in these societies than in others if the increase in the proportion of well educated people is greater than the increase in the proportion of occupational positions requiring a high level of education. This statement might be a key to the puzzles proposed by the above-mentioned studies.

Finally, these studies suggest that the amount and the structure of social mobility should be considered as consequences of a set of interacting variables. Among these variables, differential fertility should, of course, be mentioned, as was pointed out by Matras. Differential fertility influences the probability of an individual being born with a given ascriptive or origin status. Then, this individual must pass through a sequence of selection agencies, as Sorokin calls them. One of these selection agencies will, for instance, provide him with an educational level. In this respect, the variable, inequality of educational opportunities, plays an important role. The probability of an individual leaving this agency with a given level of education will be more or less related to his social origin according to the importance of this variable. Then, another "agency" will give him a job. But the kind of job obtained depends on the structure of the available jobs and on the structure of

---

*The model of this section is much more fully developed in Boudon (1973b).

117

the population of candidates for these jobs as well as on the level of education required for each category of job.

The following model is a crude attempt to generate a mathematical tool describing the mobility processes as they actually develop and, in this way, bringing the mathematics closer to the sociological theory.

## The rationale for the model

We shall suppose that a mobility process may be described as processing a population of individuals through a set of selection agencies. This concept will be given a more abstract meaning than in Sorokin's (1927) classical book, *Social Mobility*. Thus, a first agency could provide a set of children with a given level of school achievement in, say, grade 12 as a function of the social status of their fathers; a second could provide them with a level of education as a function of their school achievement in grade 12, etc. Generally, a selection agency may be represented by a turnover matrix which distributes a population of individuals in a set of output categories as a function of their position in a set of input categories.

In the following presentation, we shall consider a system with two selection agencies. The first one gives the individuals a level of education as a function of the social status of their fathers. The second one gives the same individuals an achieved social status as a function of their level of education.

In the following, we shall use the symbols $\mathbf{M}$, $\mathbf{P}$ and $\mathbf{Q}$ to describe *turnover* matrices, while $\mathbf{R}$, $\mathbf{S}$ and, in the following sections, $\mathbf{U}$ will describe *transition* matrices.

We call $\mathbf{P}_t = [p_{(t)ij}]$ the turnover matrix corresponding to the first agency. Thus, $p_{(t)ij}$ is the proportion of individuals at time $t$ whose fathers belong to the $i$th social category and who have themselves reached the $j$th educational level. In this first version of the model, the time unit is one generation, so that time $t$ means the $t$th generation. In the same way, we call $\mathbf{Q}_t = [q_{(t)ij}]$ the turnover matrix corresponding to the second selection agency. Thus, $q_{(t)ij}$ is the proportion of people of the $t$th generation with educational status $i$ and achieved occupational status $j$.

Now let $\mathbf{D}_{Pt} = \text{diag}[d_{p(t)i}]$ be a diagonal matrix, the non-zero elements of which are, in the proper order, the row totals of the turnover matrix $\mathbf{P}_t$. In the same way, $\mathbf{D}_{Qt} = \text{diag}[d_{Q(t)i}]$ is a diagonal matrix, the non-zero elements of which are the row totals of the turnover matrix $\mathbf{Q}_t$. Now

$$\mathbf{R}_t = \mathbf{D}_{Pt}^{-1}\mathbf{P}_t \tag{4.33}$$

is the transition matrix which describes the probabilities, $r_{(t)ij}$, of going to educational status $j$ from social origin category $i$ for the people of the $t$th generation. In the same way

$$\mathbf{S}_t = \mathbf{D}_{Qt}^{-1}\mathbf{Q}_t \tag{4.34}$$

is the transition matrix which describes the probabilities, $s_{(t)ij}$, of going to achieved occupational status $j$ from educational level $i$ for the individuals of the $t$th generation. The product $\mathbf{R}_t\mathbf{S}_t$, on the other hand, is the transition matrix describing the probabilities of going from a given origin status (father's status) to a given occupational status. The intergenerational turnover matrix $\mathbf{M}_t$ between generation $(t-1)$ and generation $t$ is then given by

$$\begin{aligned}
\mathbf{M}_t &= \mathbf{D}_{Pt}\mathbf{R}_t\mathbf{S}_t \\
&= \mathbf{D}_{Pt}\mathbf{D}_{Pt}^{-1}\mathbf{P}_t\mathbf{D}_{Qt}^{-1}\mathbf{Q}_t \\
&= \mathbf{P}_t\mathbf{D}_{Qt}^{-1}\mathbf{Q}_t
\end{aligned} \tag{4.35}$$

This equation was originally proposed by Carlsson (1958). It suggests, incidentally, an interesting method for deriving $\mathbf{M}_t$ when this latter matrix is not known and when $\mathbf{P}_t$, $\mathbf{D}_{Qt}$ are available. But our main interest here is to analyze the behavior of $\mathbf{M}_t$ as a function of the independent matrices $\mathbf{P}_t$, $\mathbf{D}_{Qt}$ and $\mathbf{Q}_t$, or more exactly as a function of the parameters on which these latter matrices will themselves be made dependent.

Thus, the next step is to define matrix-valued functions which will generate $\mathbf{P}_t$ and $\mathbf{Q}_t$. Let us first consider $\mathbf{P}_t$. A reasonable theory is that everybody wants to climb as high as possible on the ladder of educational levels. However, various exogenous factors force different proportions of the population to stop at the various levels. In other words, we may reasonably introduce the assumption that the proportion reaching, say, educational level $j$ at the $t$th generation is fixed by exogenous factors rather than by the will of these individuals. Thus, we assume that the proportions of educational positions at the various levels are fixed in advance and that the individuals compete to reach the highest possible level. On the other hand, we assume that the educational opportunities are unequally distributed as a function of the social origin of the subjects. Thus, the problem is to make $\mathbf{P}_t$ a function of the inequality of educational opportunity on the one hand and of the structure of the competing population and of the available educational positions on the other.

A way of constructing this function was suggested in Section 1.4, in our discussion of mobility indices. Although the procedure may be easily extended to any number of categories, let us restrict ourself to 3 ordered social and to 3 ordered educational categories, ranked from 1 (lowest level) to 3 (highest level). The detailed notation corresponding to $\mathbf{P}_t$ when this matrix is of dimension $3 \times 3$ is given in Table 4.1. Thus $p_{(t)13}$ is the proportion of the people of the $t$th generation with social origin 1 and educational level 3, while $p_{(t)1}{}^1$ is the total proportion with social origin 1 and $p_{(t)3}{}^2$ the total proportion with educational level 3.

TABLE 4.1

The notation for $\mathbf{P}_t$ with 3 social and 3 educational categories

| | | | |
|---|---|---|---|
| $\mathbf{P}_{(t)11}$ | $\mathbf{P}_{(t)12}$ | $\mathbf{P}_{(t)13}$ | $\mathbf{P}_{(t)1}{}^1$ |
| $\mathbf{P}_{(t)21}$ | $\mathbf{P}_{(t)22}$ | $\mathbf{P}_{(t)23}$ | $\mathbf{P}_{(t)2}{}^1$ |
| $\mathbf{P}_{(t)31}$ | $\mathbf{P}_{(t)32}$ | $\mathbf{P}_{(t)33}$ | $\mathbf{P}_{(t)3}{}^1$ |
| $\mathbf{P}_{(t)1}{}^2$ | $\mathbf{P}_{(t)2}{}^2$ | $\mathbf{P}_{(t)3}{}^2$ | 1 |

Let us now call $x$ a number not greater than 1 and not less than a number $x_{\min}$, itself not less than 0. (We shall return to this number $x_{\min}$ later.) Then the matrix-valued function we are looking for may take the following form

$$p_{(t)33} = x \min (p_{(t)3}{}^1, p_{(t)3}{}^2) \tag{4.36a}$$

$$p_{(t)23} = x \min (p_{(t)2}{}^1, p_{(t)3}{}^2 - p_{(t)33}) \tag{4.36b}$$

$$p_{(t)32} = x \min (p_{(t)2}{}^2, p_{(t)3}{}^1 - p_{(t)33}) \tag{4.36c}$$

$$p_{(t)22} = x \min (p_{(t)2}{}^1 - p_{(t)23}, p_{(t)2}{}^2 - p_{(t)32}) \tag{4.36d}$$

The intuitive interpretation of eqn. (4.36) is obvious: the best positions in the educational system, *i.e.* the positions at level 3 are given to the people with the highest social origin in a proportion $x$ if they are less numerous than the available educational positions in 3. If they are more numerous, they are granted a proportion $x$ of these positions. Thus, a proportion $p_{(t)3}{}^1 - p_{(t)33}$ of individuals with social origin 3 will not be located at educational level 3. Then, a proportion $x$ of these people will be granted a position at educational level 2, unless $p_{(t)3}{}^1 - p_{(t)33}$ is greater than the proportion $p_{(t)2}{}^2$ of available educational positions at level 2. In this case, the individuals with social origin 3 who have not been located in educational level 3 receive a proportion $x$ of the available positions at educational level 2, etc. The procedure is exactly the same as in Section 1.4. Then, it is supposed that the best educational positions are granted to the individuals with the best origin according to a bias measured by $x$. The remaining positions are distributed to the individuals who have not yet been located, again according to the bias $x$, up to the point where the residual positions are granted to the residual sub-population.

Obviously, $x$ cannot be smaller than $x_{\min}$, the minimum value of $x$ such that eqn. (4.36) does not generate negative figures in $\mathbf{P}_t$. This point was also discussed in Section 1.4. In the following development, we shall assume that $x$ is chosen large enough so that it is greater than $x_{\min}$.

It would, of course, be possible to extend the model by introducing several parameters describing the inequalities of educational opportunity, instead of one. Thus, we substitute $x_1$ for $x$ in eqns. (4.36a) and (4.36b) and $x_2$ for $x$ in eqns. (4.36c) and (4.36d). With $x_1 > x_2$, this means that the differential inequality of educational opportunity is greater at the upper than at the intermediate level of education. We shall, however, ignore these possible extensions.

The turnover matrix $\mathbf{Q}_t$ may, in a similar way, be treated as a function of its marginals and of a parameter, say, $y$, which in this case describes the dependence of the achieved social status on the educational level.

$$q_{(t)33} = y \min (q_{(t)3}{}^1, q_{(t)3}{}^2) \qquad (4.37a)$$

$$q_{(t)23} = y \min (q_{(t)2}{}^1, q_{(t)3}{}^2 - q_{(t)33}) \qquad (4.37b)$$

$$q_{(t)32} = y \min (q_{(t)2}{}^2, q_{(t)3}{}^1 - q_{(t)33}) \qquad (4.37c)$$

$$q_{(t)22} = y \min (q_{(t)2}{}^1 - q_{(t)23}, \; q_{(t)2}{}^2 - q_{(t)32}) \qquad (4.37d)$$

The meaning of eqn. (4.37) is the same as that of eqn. (4.36). The parameter $y$ measures the bias with which the best social positions are granted to the individuals who have a relatively better educational level. Again, it would be possible to introduce several $y$ parameters instead of one. But we shall ignore this possible extension. We shall assume $y$ greater than $y_{\min}$.

The equations (4.36) and (4.37) may be summarized in the following form.

$$\mathbf{P}_t = \mathbf{P}_t(x, \; \mathbf{p}_t{}^1, \; \mathbf{p}_t{}^2) \qquad (4.38)$$

$$\mathbf{Q}_t = \mathbf{Q}_t(y, \; \mathbf{q}_t{}^1, \; \mathbf{q}_t{}^2) \qquad (4.39)$$

where the row vector $\mathbf{p}_t{}^1 = [p_{(t)i}{}^1]$ describes the row total of $\mathbf{P}_t$ and $\mathbf{p}_t{}^2 = [p_{(t)i}{}^2]$ its column totals, while $\mathbf{q}_t{}^1 = [q_{(t)i}{}^1]$ and $\mathbf{q}_t{}^2 = [q_{(t)i}{}^2]$ describe respectively the row and column totals of $\mathbf{Q}_t$.

*Introducing the effect of differential fertility and of changes in the educational and social structures*

Let us now define the following diagonal matrices.

$\mathbf{F}_t = \operatorname{diag} [f_i/f_t]$ is a differential fertility matrix, the $i$th non-zero element of which describes the ratio of the reproduction rate of the $i$th social class to the overall reproduction rate.

$\mathbf{E}_t = \operatorname{diag} [e_i/e_t]$ is a matrix describing the changes in the educational structure from one generation to the next; $e_i$ is the net rate of increase at the $i$th level of education, $e_t$ the overall increase. Then, the $i$th non-zero element of the matrix describes the ratio of the increase at the $i$th educational level to the overall rate of increase.

$\mathbf{V}_t = \operatorname{diag} [v_i/v_t]$ is a diagonal matrix ·describing the changes in the social structure from one generation to the next; $v_i$ is the net rate of increase of the $i$th social category, $v_t$ the overall increase. Then, the $i$th non-zero element of the matrix is the ratio of the rate of increase of the $i$th social category to the overall rate of increase of the population of social positions.

Let us see how the process develops with time. Call $\mathbf{q}_0{}^2$ the row vector describing the distribution of the initial population according to social status. For the following generation, the distribution $\mathbf{p}_1{}^1 = [p_{(1)i}{}^1]$ for the ascribed family statuses will be

$$p_1{}^1 = q_0{}^2 F_1 \qquad (4.40)$$

Let, on the other hand, $q_0{}^1$ be a row vector describing the distribution of the initial population according to educational level. For the following generation, the structure of the available educational positions will be

$$p_1{}^2 = q_0{}^1 E_1 \qquad (4.41)$$

Then

$$P_1 = P_1(x, p_1{}^1, p_1{}^2)$$

$$= P_1(x, q_0{}^2 F_1, q_0{}^1 E_1) \qquad (4.42)$$

Between the generation corresponding to our initial population and the next generation (generation 1), the social structure (distribution of social statuses) into which the people belonging to generation 1 will be integrated will have changed. At time 1 it will be

$$q_1{}^2 = q_0{}^2 V_1 \qquad (4.43)$$

Then

$$Q_1 = Q_1(y, q_1{}^1, q_1{}^2)$$

$$= Q_1(y, q_1{}^1, q_0{}^2 V_1) \qquad (4.44)$$

The vector $q_1{}^1$ includes, as we recall, the row totals of $Q_1$. But these row totals are also the column totals of $P_1$. Thus

$$q_1{}^1 = p_1{}^2 \qquad (4.45)$$

Substituting eqns. (4.41) and (4.45) into eqn. (4.44), we obtain

$$Q_1 = Q_1(y, p_1{}^2, q_0{}^2 V_1)$$

$$= Q_1(y, p_0{}^2 E_1, q_0{}^2 V_1) \qquad (4.46)$$

Generally

$$P_t = P_t(x, p_t{}^1, p_t{}^2)$$

$$= P_t(x, q_0{}^2 F_1 F_2 \cdots F_t, q_0{}^1 E_1 E_2 \cdots E_t) \qquad (4.47a)$$

$$Q_t = Q_t(y, q_t{}^1, q_t{}^2)$$

$$= Q_t(y, q_0{}^1 E_1 E_2 \cdots E_t, q_0{}^2 V_1 V_2 \cdots V_t) \qquad (4.47b)$$

Finally, the intergenerational mobility turnover table relating the actual status of the people belonging to the $t$th generation to the status of their fathers will be, by eqns. (4.35) and (4.47)

$$\mathbf{M}_t = \mathbf{P}_t \mathbf{D}_{Qt}^{-1} \mathbf{Q}_t$$

$$= \mathbf{P}_t(x, \mathbf{q}_0^2 \mathbf{F}_1 \mathbf{F}_2 \ \cdots \ \mathbf{F}_t, \mathbf{q}_0^1 \mathbf{E}_1 \mathbf{E}_2 \ \cdots \ \mathbf{E}_t)$$

$$\times \mathbf{D}_{Qt}^{-1} \mathbf{Q}_t(y, \mathbf{q}_0^1 \mathbf{E}_1 \mathbf{E}_2 \ \cdots \ \mathbf{E}_t, \mathbf{q}_0^2 \mathbf{V}_1 \mathbf{V}_2 \ \cdots \ \mathbf{V}_t) \qquad (4.48)$$

This is obviously a rather complicated model. Its mathematical analysis (*i.e.* the general analysis of its behavior as a function of its localization in the parametric space) is clearly difficult. This difficulty derives from the large number of parameters introduced

(1) $\mathbf{q}_0^1$ and $\mathbf{q}_0^2$, the initial distributions with respect to the educational and social statuses,

(2) $x$ and $y$, and

(3) the $f_i$'s, $e_i$'s and $v_i$'s.

It must, however, be realized that, in spite of its complexity, the actual mobility processes of the model are highly simplified. First, the $f_i$'s, $e_i$'s and $v_i$'s are supposed constant through time. Then, $x$ is unique, whereas a matrix of order, say $3 \times 3$, has 4 degrees of freedom when the marginals are fixed. The same holds for $y$. On the other hand, the model assumes a discontinuous succession of generations, *i.e.*, say, that all the sons are born at the beginning of a generational period and then simultaneously compete, first for an educational level, then for a social status. This is clearly very unrealistic. The model can, however, be rather easily corrected for this latter point, as we shall see below. Finally, it assumes an influence of family status on the level of education and of the level of education on the achieved status, while it is known that family status will still influence the achieved status even if the level of education is controlled. In other words, the model assumes a causal structure which is simpler than the structures which may be found in the statistical studies of mobility (*e.g.* Blau and Duncan (1967)).

*Uses of the model*

The main interest of the model is theoretical rather than empirical. It belongs to a type of model which is often used in economics, but more rarely in sociology. It may be used, for instance, to analyze the effect on the mobility process of an increasing distortion between the educational and the social structure. The effects of differential fertility on the mobility processes may be investigated to predict the effect of a given educational policy (*e.g.* faster increase in the size of educational level 2 than of educational level 3 as compared to the converse) on the mobility of the various social classes. Generally speaking, the model assumes that the structure of the mobility processes is a complex consequence of the interactions of a number of variables: (a) The level of inequality of educational opportunity, (b) differential fertility, (c) changes in the occupational and in the educational structure and (d) the strength of the relationship between educational level and expected social status. It may be used to investigate the effects of any given combinations of these variables.

Empirically, the potential uses of the model are numerous. But they are confronted with the scarcity of long series of intergenerational mobility data. Thus, with a set of relevant information, it is possible to try to solve the equations of the model for some unknown parameters, for instance $x$ and $y$. But the main difficulty for possible empirical applications of this model lies in the length of the generational time unit used. Thus, the time series generated cannot be easily compared to actual series of data. We shall see below how this weakness can be eliminated in more refined versions of the model.

But a model need not necessarily "fit" empirical data to be useful. It may also be a tool which allows the derivation of statements which are not possible intuitively. We have such a situation here. It is impossible to deduce intuitively the effects on social mobility resulting from a given combination of the parameters. For this reason it is, reciprocally, difficult to understand the meaning of some sets of mobility data, which often seem puzzling or even contradictory. Let us consider, for instance, the case of a comparison between two mobility matrices. We have seen in the previous chapters that it is necessary to make a distinction between exchange (or pure) and structural mobility. But it must be realized that this concept of structural mobility is very unsatisfactory from a theoretical point of view. Indeed, structural mobility, in the sense used in the previous chapters, is more precisely that fraction of the actual structural mobility we are able to identify when our information is limited to mobility tables. Thus, this concept is a product of the limitation of the data usually available rather than of a satisfactory mobility theory. Indeed, another fraction of this structural mobility results from the effect of the differential fertility. Still another results from the possible inadequacy of the relationship between the social and educational structures. Thus, a comparison between two mobility tables, to be completely satisfactory from a theoretical point of view, would have to isolate and to compare these different kinds of structural mobility.

Thus, a prime function of the type of model considered here is to clarify the complicated interaction of the structural factors which, taken together, account for mobility. In this sense, it is a theoretical model of the type used, say, in economics more than in sociology. The main aim of these (see, for instance, the mathematical theory of business cycles) is to explore the consequences that result from distinct combinations of independent and intervening variables, rather than to "reproduce" a given set of data.

The model could, however, in spite of its theoretical orientation, be applied directly to empirical problems, such as the comparison of intergenerational mobility matrices. Let us suppose, for instance, that we have at our disposal, besides the usual mobility matrices, relevant information on the $f_i$'s, $e_i$'s and $s_i$'s, as well as on the distribution of the respondents according to educational level. Then, we may try to solve eqns. (4.42) and (4.46) respectively for $x$ and $y$. If this solution is possible, each mobility matrix will be represented as a function of a set of parameters. Then, the comparison of the mobility matrices will become a comparison of these parameters, and consequently a comparison of the relative contribution of the various structural sources of mobility. This procedure would obviously be much more satisfactory than the usual index-building procedures, since it rests on a genuine theory, while the theories on which most indices are grounded are strongly determined by the limitations of the data.

*An application of the model*

Let us suppose we are interested in the effect of the structure of educational growth on differential educational mobility. By educational mobility, we mean the probability of a youngster, say, from social class 1 reaching educational level 2 or 3 rather than 1, etc. The theoretical question we shall explore is whether a growth structure of the educational system characterized by a higher rate of growth at the third than at the second educational level has,

126

other things being equal, a positive or a negative effect on the educational mobility of the lowest social class.

We shall make the following assumptions.

(1) $F_t = V_t = I$. This is a simplifying assumption. It states that there is neither differential fertility nor differential growth of the social structure.

(2) $e_3 > e_2 > 1$. The rate of growth of the highest educational level is greater than the rate of growth of the second level. This latter level may be, for instance, interpreted as the higher education level, while the former represents the secondary level.

(3) $x$ is large. There is a strong inequality of educational opportunity.

(4) $y$ is large. A high educational level is required to obtain the higher social positions.

(5) At the initial time, the proportion of people in a social category is greater, the lower the category; the same holds for educational level; on the other hand the mean of the educational distribution is lower than the mean of the social distribution.

These assumptions amount to a local exploration of the model in a region of the parametric space. While assumption (1) is unrealistic and should be removed at a later stage, the others picture quite realistically the situation of, say, many European countries in recent decades.

The first stage of the analysis consists in determining the phases of the process. Going back to eqn. (4.36), we notice that the values of some variables on which the functions *min* are defined will change through time according to assumption (2). Then, the

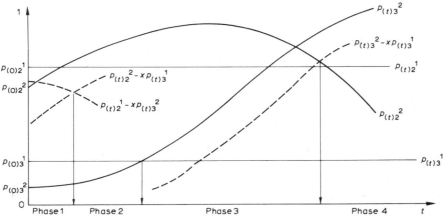

Figure 4.1. Graphical analysis of eqn (4.36)

127

variables with minimum value will change. Thus, assumption (5) can state that at the initial time, $p_{(0)3}^{1}$, the proportion of people in social class 3 will be greater than $p_{(0)3}^{2}$, the proportion of people with educational level 3. But the former quantity will become smaller with time, when the increase at educational level 3 is sufficient.

Probably the easiest way to analyze the behavior of the process is graphically. In Fig. 4.1, the points corresponding to $p_{(0)2}^{1}$ and $p_{(0)3}^{1}$ (proportions in social classes 2 and 3) as well as to $p_{(0)2}^{2}$ and $p_{(0)3}^{2}$ (proportions with educational levels 2 and 3) have been located according to assumption (5) on the initial conditions. Then, we have drawn the curves $p_{(t)2}^{1}$ and $p_{(t)3}^{1}$, which are parallel to the $x$-axis since no differential changes have been assumed in the social structure. Finally, we have drawn the curves $p_{(t)2}^{2}$ and $p_{(t)3}^{2}$ (proportions with levels of education 2 and 3 and represented their general form as derived from the initial assumptions and from assumption (2), i.e. $e_3 > e_2 > 1$.

The graph shows that the process has several phases. In the first phase, the equations are

$$p_{(t)33} = x \min (p_{(t)3}^{1}, p_{(t)3}^{2}) = x p_{(t)3}^{2} \qquad (4.49a)$$

$$p_{(t)23} = x \min (p_{(t)2}^{1}, p_{(t)3}^{2} - p_{(t)33})$$

$$= x(p_{(t)3}^{2} - p_{(t)33}) \qquad (4.49b)$$

$$p_{(t)32} = x \min (p_{(t)2}^{2}, p_{(t)3}^{1} - p_{(t)33})$$

$$= x(p_{(t)3}^{1} - p_{(t)33}) \qquad (4.49c)$$

$$p_{(t)22} = x \min (p_{(t)2}^{1} - p_{(t)23}, p_{(t)2}^{2} - p_{(t)32})$$

$$= x(p_{(t)2}^{2} - p_{(t)32}) \qquad (4.49d)$$

Then, in a second phase, eqn. (4.59d) is reformulated as

$$p_{(t)22} = x(p_{(t)2}^{1} - p_{(t)23}) \qquad (4.49d')$$

This happens when

$$p_{(t)2}^{2} - p_{(t)32} > p_{(t)2}^{1} - p_{(t)23}$$

i.e. when

$$p_{(t)2}^{2} - x(p_{(t)3}^{1} - p_{(t)33}) > p_{(t)2}^{1} - x(p_{(t)3}^{2} - p_{(t)33})$$

128

or when

$$p_{(t)2}{}^2 - xp_{(t)3}{}^1 > p_{(t)2}{}^1 - xp_{(t)3}{}^2$$

In a third phase, eqn. (4.49a) is reformulated as

$$p_{(t)33} = xp_{(t)3}{}^1 \qquad\qquad (4.49a')$$

Then, in a very advanced stage of the process, eqn. (4.49b) is also reformulated as

$$p_{(t)32} = xp_{(t)2}{}^2 \qquad\qquad (4.49c')$$

But we may ignore this fourth phase in which a majority of people reach the highest educational level.

Let us now introduce the following definitions

$$G_{(t)ij} = p_{(t)ij} - p_{(t-1)ij} \qquad\qquad (4.50)$$

Thus, $G_{(t)ij}$ is the increase (decrease) between $(t-1)$ and $t$ in the proportion of people who come from social class $i$ and reach educational level $j$. In the same way

$$G_{(t)j}{}^2 = p_{(t)j}{}^2 - p_{(t-1)j}{}^2 \qquad\qquad (4.51)$$

is the increase (decrease) between $(t-1)$ and $t$, in the proportion of educational positions of level $j$. $G_{(t)i}{}^1$ is defined in the same way and describes the increase between $(t-1)$ and $t$ in the proportion of social positions of level $i$. But since the social structure is assumed not to change

$$G_{(t)i}{}^1 = 0 \qquad\qquad (4.52)$$

On the other hand, we obviously have

$$\sum_j G_{(t)j}{}^2 = 0 \qquad\qquad (4.53)$$

$$\sum_i G_{(t)ij} = G_{(t)j}{}^2 \qquad\qquad (4.54)$$

We shall now study the $G_{(t)ij}$'s, *i.e.* for social class $i$, the increase (decrease) in the proportion of educational positions of level $j$.

*Phase 1*

In this first phase, by eqns. (4.49a, b, c, d)

$$G_{(t)33} = xG_{(t)3}{}^2 \qquad\qquad (4.55a)$$

$$G_{(t)23} = x(G_{(t)3}{}^2 - xG_{(t)3}{}^2) = x(1-x)G_{(t)3}{}^2 \qquad\qquad (4.55b)$$

129

$$G_{(t)32} = -x^2 G_{(t)3}{}^2 \qquad\qquad (4.55c)$$

$$G_{(t)22} = x(G_{(t)2}{}^2 - x^2 G_{(t)3}{}^2) \qquad\qquad (4.55d)$$

Thus, $100x\%$ of the increase in educational positions at level 3 goes to class 3, $100x(1-x)\%$ to class 2 and the rest, *i.e.* $100(1-x)^2\%$ to class 1. On the other hand, the proportion of youngsters from class 3 who reach educational level 2 declines and they are replaced by youngsters from classes 2 and 3. The youngsters of class 2 take a proportion $x$ of the new positions at educational level 2 while those of class 1 take a proportion $(1-x)$. Moreover, they get, respectively, proportions $x$ and $(1-x)$ of the positions at level 2 not used by youngsters of a higher class.

*Phase 2*

Equations (4.55a, b, c) hold for this second phase. But (4.55d) must be replaced since (4.49d') has to be substituted for (4.49d).

$$\begin{aligned}G_{(t)22} &= -x G_{(t)23} \\ &= -x^2(1-x)G_{(t)3}{}^2 \qquad\qquad (4.55d')\end{aligned}$$

The number of people from class 2 reaching only the second level of education decreases, so that all the new positions created at this level go to class 1. However, as can be seen on the graph of Fig. 4.1, the proportion of these new positions increases less during the second stage of the process. The proportion of new positions of level 3 which go to class 1 is still very low (since $x$ has been supposed high), *i.e.* $(1-x)^2$.

*Phase 3*

Since eqn. (4.49a') has now to be substituted for eqn. (4.49a), eqn. (4.55a) must be replaced by

$$G_{(t)33} = x G_{(t)3}{}^1 = 0 \qquad\qquad (4.55a')$$

This leads to

$$G_{(t)23} = x G_{(t)3}{}^2 \qquad\qquad (4.55b')$$

$$G_{(t)32} = 0 \qquad\qquad (4.55c')$$

$$G_{(t)22} = x(-x G_{(t)3}{}^2) \qquad\qquad (4.55d'')$$

130

Thus, in this third phase, a proportion $x$ of the new positions at educational level 3 go to people from class 2 and a proportion $(1-x)$ to class 1. On the other hand, class 1 will receive all the new positions created at the second level. But, sometime during phase 3, there will be (see Fig. 4.1) a decrease rather than an increase in the proportion of second-level positions. Since, on the other hand, the proportion of new positions of level 3 which are returned to class 1 is low, $G_{(t)11}$, the proportion of people from class 1 who reach only the first level of education, will eventually increase.

Hence, we reach the conclusion that a tremendous increase in the rates of school attendance is not incompatible with a stagnation or even a regression in the educational mobility of the lower classes, when $e_3 > e_2$, *i.e.* when the rate of increase is greater at the upper educational level. Perhaps the model explains to some extent the fact that in most industrial societies we observe both a stagnation of educational mobility of the lower classes and a larger growth rate at the upper educational level.

This elementary application of the model aims at illustrating its potential usefulness at a theoretical level. Other applications may be devised. On the other hand, more refined forms may be developed, as we shall see in the next sub-section and in the last section of this chapter.

*Pseudo-cohort version of the model*

Let us suppose an intergenerational mobility matrix with a sufficiently large population. The population of respondents may be partitioned into age groups. Let us assume the presence of relevant information on the fertility rates, as well as on the changes in the educational and social structures. Then, we may use the previous model separately for each age group. The age groups will be exposed to distinct states of the social and educational structure. The equations of the model are then solved for $x$ and $y$ for each age group separately. Finally, the sum of the mobility matrices corresponding to each of the age groups is verified to reproduce correctly the overall mobility matrix.

The basic equation of this pseudo-cohort model is the following (for the sake of simplicity, we shall consider one generation and $(m+1)$ age groups numbered $0, 1, ..., i, ..., m$)

$$M = \sum_{i=0}^{m} M_i$$

$$= \sum_{i=0}^{m} P_i D_{Qi}^{-1} Q_i$$

$$= \sum_{i=0}^{m} P_i(x_i, p_i^1, p_0^2 E_0 E_1 E_2 \ldots E_i) D_{Qi}^{-1}$$

$$\times Q_i(y_i, p_0^2 E_0 E_1 E_2 \ldots E_i, p_0^1 V_0 V_1 V_2 \ldots V_i)$$

$$\text{(with } E_0 = V_0 = I) \qquad (4.56)$$

This equation is slightly different from eqn. (4.48). The age groups are numbered from 0 to $m$. The vector $p_i^1$ is the distribution of the $i$th age group as a function of social origin; $p_0^2 E_0 E_1 E_2 \ldots E_i$, the distribution of the $i$th age group according to the level of education; $p_0^1 V_0 V_1 V_2 \ldots V_i$ its distribution according to achieved social status. On the other hand, $x$ and $y$ become dependent on age group and consequently, on time. Finally, $M$ is the mobility matrix, predicted from the model, which is to be compared with the observed intergenerational mobility matrix. The survey or census data from which the mobility matrix is extracted, are assumed to allow for an estimation of the parameters $e_i$ and $v_i$. Of course, it is supposed that the functions $P_i$ and $Q_i$ are defined by eqns. (4.36) and (4.37).

The interest of this pseudo-cohort model is that it allows for a comparison between turnover matrices grounded on a theory of the mobility process. The comparison will thus tell us not only *to what extent* the matrices differ, but also *why* they differ.

### 4.4. A true cohort socio-demographic model

Matras (1966) has suggested a very interesting adaptation to mobility analysis of a demographic model proposed by Keyfitz (1964). This model has the advantage of introducing a birth and death process and of stratifying the mobility processes by age. This is undoubtedly a great step forward when compared with most mobility models which generally deal with fictitious populations considered as both closed and homogeneous with respect to

132

age. Thus Matras' suggestion is certainly of great potential use for mobility analysis.

*Introducing age, fertility and social status into a transition matrix*

Let us suppose that a population may be partitioned into social statuses at each age. For the younger people, this status is, of course, that of their parents. Then call $n_{(t)ij}$ the number of people who, at time $t$ (say, year $t$), have age $i$ and status $j$, rank these quantities in a lexicographic order and call $n_t$ the resulting row vector.

$$\mathbf{n}_t = [n_{(t)11}, n_{(t)12}, \ldots, n_{(t)1\sigma}; n_{(t)21}, n_{(t)22}, \ldots,$$

$$n_{(t)2\sigma}; \ldots; n_{(t)g1}, n_{(t)g2}, \ldots, n_{(t)g\sigma}] \tag{4.57}$$

where $g$ is the number of age groups. Then define a set of matrices in the following way

$\mathbf{R}_i = \text{diag}[r_{ij}]$, as a set of $g$ diagonal matrices, where $r_{ij}$ is the probability that a male from age group $i$ and social status $j$ sires a son who survives;

$\mathbf{U}_i = [u_{ijk}]$ as a set of $(g-1)$ matrices, where $u_{ijk}$ is the probability that a male from age group $i$ and social category $j$ survives and obtains social status $k$ in the year.

Let us then combine these sub-matrices into a matrix $\mathbf{T}$ so that the $\mathbf{R}_i$'s become the first column of $\mathbf{T}$, while the $\mathbf{U}_i$'s are located in the $i$th row and $(i+1)$th column

$$\mathbf{T} = \begin{bmatrix} \mathbf{R}_1 & \mathbf{U}_1 & 0 & 0 & \ldots & 0 \\ \mathbf{R}_2 & 0 & \mathbf{U}_2 & 0 & \ldots & 0 \\ \mathbf{R}_3 & 0 & 0 & \mathbf{U}_3 & \ldots & 0 \\ \hdotsfor{6} \\ \mathbf{R}_{(g-1)} & 0 & 0 & 0 & \ldots & \mathbf{U}_{(g-1)} \\ \mathbf{R}_g & 0 & 0 & 0 & \ldots & 0 \end{bmatrix} \tag{4.58}$$

It is readily verified that

$$\mathbf{n}_t \mathbf{T} = \mathbf{n}_{(t+1)} \tag{4.59}$$

In other words, postmultiplying $\mathbf{n}_t$, the distribution of the population at time $t$, by $\mathbf{T}$, gives the distribution of the population at

133

time $(t + 1)$, *i.e.* one time unit later. It must be noted that a number $(g - 1)$ of $\mathbf{U}_i$ matrices has been assumed. Indeed, $g$ is the oldest age group and $u_{ijk}$ with $i = (g - 1)$, *i.e.* an element of the $\mathbf{U}_{(g-1)}$ matrix, is the probability of a male with age $(g - 1)$ going from status $i$ to status $k$ and surviving, that is reaching the last age group $g$.

If we are prepared to assume the stationarity of $\mathbf{T}$, *i.e.* its independence through time, eqn. (4.59) generates what may be called a stratified Markov chain with

$$\mathbf{n}_0 \mathbf{T} = \mathbf{n}_1 \qquad\qquad\qquad (4.60a)$$

$$\mathbf{n}_1 \mathbf{T} = \mathbf{n}_0 \mathbf{T}^2 = \mathbf{n}_2 \qquad\qquad\qquad (4.60b)$$

$$\cdots\cdots\cdots\cdots\cdots$$

$$\mathbf{n}_t \mathbf{T} = \mathbf{n}_0 \mathbf{T}^{(t+1)} = \mathbf{n}_{(t+1)} \qquad\qquad\qquad (4.60c)$$

In contrast to the case of ordinary Markov chains where the $(t+1)$th power of the transition matrix is a $(t+1)$-step transition matrix, the matrix $\mathbf{T}$ raised to the $(t+1)$th power is not easily interpretable.

On the other hand, the model can obviously be adapted as a useful tool for the analysis of intergenerational mobility matrices. Let us suppose we have observed an intergenerational mobility matrix and that we know the ages of the respondents. Let us, on the other hand, assume a proportion $p_{mj}$ of those who have age $m$ and report that their father had social status $j$. Describe these proportions by the row vector $\mathbf{p}_m = [p_{mj}]$. In the same way, the vectors $\mathbf{p}_{(m+1)}, \ldots, \mathbf{p}_g$ will describe the distribution of the respondents with ages $(m+1), \ldots, g$ as a function of the social status of their fathers. Then

$$\mathbf{p}_m \mathbf{U}_1 \mathbf{U}_2 \cdots \mathbf{U}_{(m-1)}$$

is a row vector describing the distribution of the current social statuses of the people of age $m$. In the same way

$$\bar{\mathbf{p}}_{(m+1)} \mathbf{U}_1 \mathbf{U}_2 \cdots \mathbf{U}_m$$

$$\cdots\cdots\cdots\cdots\cdots$$

$$\mathbf{p}_g \mathbf{U}_1 \mathbf{U}_2 \cdots \mathbf{U}_{(g-1)}$$

describes the distribution of the respondents with ages $(m+1), \ldots, g$

134

at the time of the observation. Let us now suppose the proportion of respondents with age $m$ in the sample to be $a_m$, the proportion with age $(m + 1)$, $a_{(m+1)}$, ..., the proportion with age $g$, $a_g$ and organize these proportions into a set of scalar matrices $\mathbf{D}_m$ = diag$[a_m]$, $\mathbf{D}_{(m+1)}$ = diag$[a_{(m+1)}]$, ..., $\mathbf{D}_g$ = diag$[a_g]$, each of order $\sigma \times \sigma$. Then

$$\mathbf{D}_m \mathbf{U}_1 \mathbf{U}_2 \cdots \mathbf{U}_{(m-1)} + \mathbf{D}_{(m+1)} \mathbf{U}_1 \mathbf{U}_2 \cdots \mathbf{U}_m + \cdots + \mathbf{D}_g \mathbf{U}_1 \mathbf{U}_2 \cdots \mathbf{U}_{(g-1)}$$

is the intergenerational transition matrix corresponding to the observer population. Let us assume, for the sake of simplicity, that the group reporting each parental status has the same age distribution. In order to obtain the corresponding turnover matrix, we must organize the elements of the row vector

$$\sum_m^g a_m \mathbf{p}_m = \sum_m^g [a_m p_{m1}, a_m p_{m2}, \ldots, a_m p_{m\sigma}] = \mathbf{p}_m \qquad (4.61)$$

into a diagonal matrix, say $\mathbf{D}_w$. Then

$$\mathbf{M} = \mathbf{D}_w (\mathbf{D}_m \mathbf{U}_1 \mathbf{U}_2 \cdots \mathbf{U}_{(m-1)} + \mathbf{D}_{(m+1)} \mathbf{U}_1 \mathbf{U}_2 \cdots \mathbf{U}_m$$

$$+ \mathbf{D}_g \mathbf{U}_1 \mathbf{U}_2 \cdots \mathbf{U}_{(g-1)}) \qquad (4.62)$$

is the intergenerational turnover matrix of proportions corresponding to the observed population.

Thus, if we know the ages of the individuals in a sample of respondents, as well as their current status and their father's status, with information from other sources about $\mathbf{U}_1, \mathbf{U}_2, \ldots, \mathbf{U}_g$, we may try to reproduce the observed turnover matrix using eqn. (4.62).

*An adaptation of the model to the analysis of educational mobility*

In the presentation of model (4.59), Matras says
"Practically it would seem necessary to make some simplifying assumptions concerning timing of births relative to mobility"
Coleman (1971) has done this in an application of model (4.59). He is interested, not in the actual demographic births, but in the fact that a child is born for the educational system. He locates this educational birth at 14, the age when in the American educational system, a youngster may be directed towards different types of school careers (general *vs.* vocational education). Then, the educa-

135

tional age is equal to the actual age minus 14. The time unit is one year. On the other hand, Coleman considers 4 distinct types of statuses: college preparatory education, vocational education, blue-collar job, white-collar job.

As a result of this timing, the $R_i$ matrices of the original model are no longer necessarily diagonal. The definition of these matrices is now

$R_i = [r_{ij}]$, a set of matrices describing the probabilities $r_{ij}$ that a male from educational age group $i$ (actual age minus 14) and status $j$ sires a son who survives until educational age 0, *i.e.* until 14. These matrices are no longer diagonal, since the 14 year old youngsters need not have the same status as their father, while in the general presentation of the model of the previous sub-section, the new-born children had, necessarily, the status of their father.

*A dynamic version of the model or a cohort version of the model of Section 4.3*

This model has two shortcomings in providing a realistic description of social mobility and an acceptable sociological theory of the causes of mobility: (1) the stationarity of $T$ which may, in many cases, be questionable, especially when educational statuses are considered; (2) the implicit causal ordering which makes social structures dependent on the transition mobility probabilities.

The rationale for the model presented in Section 4.3 may be used to obtain a synthesis between this latter model and model (4.59), both of these being steps towards a more satisfactory description of social mobility.

This synthesis may be created by making the sub-matrices $U_i$ which appear in eqn. (4.58), or rather the corresponding turnover matrices a function of their marginals, and by making these marginals a function of time, as in the model of Section 4.3.

Thus, let us consider the people who have age $i$ when our observations begin (first observation year) and call $U_{0i}$ the transition matrix $[u_{(0)ijk}]$ giving the probabilities of going from status $j$ to status $k$ for the individuals belonging to the $i$th age group at time 0. Then call $P_{0i}$ the corresponding turnover matrix and, respectively, $p_{(0)i}^1$ and $p_{(0)i}^2$ the row and column totals of $P_{0i}$. As in the model of Section 4.3, $P_{0i}$ will be made a function of its marginals and of one or of several inequality parameters. If we choose to restrict ourselves to a single parameter, say $x$,

$$\mathbf{P}_{0i} = \mathbf{P}_{0i}(x, \, \mathbf{p}_{(0)i}{}^1, \, \mathbf{p}_{(0)i}{}^2) \qquad (4.63)$$

where the function $\mathbf{P}(\ \ )$ is defined exactly as in eqns. (4.36) or (4.37).

The next step is to make the marginals a function of time: let $s_{ij}$ be the rate of growth of the number of social positions with status $j$ for the people of age $i$ in one year and $s_{i1}$ be the overall rate of growth of the number of positions held by people with age $i$ between time 0 and time 1. Then, the diagonal matrix $\mathbf{S}_{i1} = \mathrm{diag}[s_{ij}/s_{i1}]$ is such that

$$\mathbf{p}_{(1)i}{}^2 = \mathbf{p}_{(0)i}{}^2 \mathbf{S}_{i1} \qquad (4.64)$$

Generally

$$\mathbf{p}_{(t)i}{}^2 = \mathbf{p}_{(0)i}{}^2 \mathbf{S}_{i1} \cdots \mathbf{S}_{it} \qquad (4.65)$$

where $\mathbf{p}_{(t)i}{}^2$ is the distribution according to status of the positions which the people with age $i$ will fill at time $t$.

The vector $\mathbf{p}_{(0)i}{}^1$ describes, on the other hand, as we recall, the row totals of $\mathbf{P}_{0i}$. In the same way, $\mathbf{p}_{(1)i}{}^1$ includes the row totals of $\mathbf{P}_{1i}$, the turnover matrix for the people with age $i$ at time 1. What is now the relationship giving $\mathbf{p}_{(1)i}{}^1$ as a function of some initial distribution? Obviously, those people with age $i$ who compete at time 1 for a new social status are those with age $(i-1)$ at time 0. Now, the distribution of these people according to status is $\mathbf{p}_{(0)(i-1)}{}^2$. Thus

$$\mathbf{p}_{(1)i}{}^1 = \mathbf{p}_{(0)(i-1)}{}^2 \qquad (4.66)$$

And, generally,

$$\mathbf{p}_{(t)i}{}^1 = \mathbf{p}_{(t-1)(i-1)}{}^2$$
$$= \mathbf{p}_{(0)(i-1)}{}^2 \mathbf{S}_{(i-1),1} \mathbf{S}_{(i-1),t} \qquad (4.67)$$

Thus

$$\mathbf{P}_{ti} = \mathbf{P}_{ti}(x, \, \mathbf{p}_{(t)i}{}^1, \, \mathbf{p}_{(t)i}{}^2)$$
$$= \mathbf{P}_{ti}(x, \, \mathbf{p}_{(0)(i-1)}{}^2 \mathbf{S}_{(i-1),1} \cdots \mathbf{S}_{(i-1),t},$$
$$\mathbf{p}_{(0)i}{}^2 \mathbf{S}_{i1} \cdots \mathbf{S}_{it}) \qquad (4.68)$$

An adequate transformation gives then the transition matrix $\mathbf{U}_{ti}$ derived from the turnover matrix $\mathbf{P}_{ti}$. And we have finally the dynamic version of the Matras model

137

$$n_{(t+1)} = n_t T_t \tag{4.69}$$

with

$$T_t = \begin{bmatrix} R_1 & U_{t1} & 0 & 0 & \dots & 0 \\ R_2 & 0 & U_{t2} & 0 & \dots & 0 \\ R_2 & 0 & 0 & U_{t3} & \dots & 0 \\ \multicolumn{6}{c}{\dots\dots\dots\dots\dots\dots\dots\dots\dots\dots\dots\dots} \\ R_{(g-1)} & 0 & 0 & 0 & \dots & U_{t,(g-1)} \\ R_g & 0 & 0 & 0 & \dots & 0 \end{bmatrix} \tag{4.70}$$

In summary, the model formalizes conceptually the following set of assumptions.

(1) The individuals of each cohort are in a situation of competition.

(2) At each time unit, they pass through an orientation agency which eventually provides them with a new status.

(3) The position they reach at the end of the time unit depends on the position they had at the beginning, since the orientation agencies are inequalitarian.

(4) A cohort with age $i$ at time $t$ and a cohort with age $i$ at time, say, $(t+1)$, may not meet the same structural conditions since the distribution of the available positions at the end of the time unit may have changed.

(5) A cohort with age $i$ at time $t$ may not meet the same conditions as a cohort with age $i$ at time $(t+1)$ since the distribution of these cohorts according to their status at the beginning of the period may differ.

These statements may be found, in a more or less similar form, in the classical theories of social mobility, such as Sorokin's theory. The Matras model of this section, the model of Section 4.3 and the synthesis which may be derived from these models may thus be considered as steps towards a closer relationship between sociological theory and empirical research on one hand, and model-building on the other.

Finally, it must be noted that the models of this section have been presented in a general form. Their application to empirical as well as to theoretical problems would require adaptations and specifications. The complexity of these models and particularly of the last one make these possible specifications very numerous.

138

# Concluding Remarks

Until now, mathematical models have had a limited influence on social mobility theory and research. The present review shows, however, that this situation is very likely. to change in the near future. Probably the stage has now been reached where empirical and theoretical research on mobility will be increasingly difficult without mathematics.

Chapter 1 has shown that a revision of the comparative mobility findings in the light of mathematical criticism of the indices which are currently being used would perhaps lead to interesting results. The following three chapters have tried to show that we have now progressed far from the first formalization attempts to represent a mobility process as an ordinary Markov chain. The mathematical models proposed in the last few years are now, by the complexity of their assumptions, much closer to an acceptable representation of the mobility processes.

With further progress, the mathematical mobility models will start to play a crucial role.

(1) They will contribute to developing more adequate theories in the field of social mobility. Consider, for instance, the case of Sorokin's theory. It embodies a set of undoubtedly true statements. However, as long as the theory is expressed in a purely verbal way, it is impossible to deduce the consequences that result from these statements taken together. Shifts in the educational structure, shifts in the social structure, shifts in the way the family conceives its selection function, etc. are factors that all have an influence on mobility. At the verbal level it is, however, impossible to go beyond a simple enumeration of these factors. In order to

explore the complex consequences that result from the action of this system of factors, mathematical models are needed.

(2) The development of mathematical models will, on the other hand, contribute to a better interaction between theory and empirical research.

Empirical research in the field of mobility has been overwhelmingly oriented towards a description rather than towards an explanation of the mobility processes. One of its main subjects is comparative mobility. The chief problem in this area may be formulated in the following way: to what extent is mobility greater in one country than in another? Greater at this time than at another? But the most interesting problem when comparing mobility matrices is to know how and why they are different rather than to know to what extent they are different. The former questions can, however, only be answered by showing that the matrices may be generated by some formalized underlying process. Otherwise, we have to be content with choosing a reasonable index and trying to determine to what extent the matrices differ. The explanation of the eventual difference or lack of difference will then take the form of a superimposed verbal theory.

A second main subject of empirical research in the field of mobility is the statistical analysis of the relationship between social status and a set of independent variables. But the most sophisticated regression analysis will never be a substitute for a real explanation of why a set of individuals has a given social status. Their current status is, in fact, the complex product of a sequence of orientations through selection agencies, as Sorokin would say. Now, the structural characteristics of these selection agencies change as a function of exogenous and endogenous variables. Thus, a correlation or even a partial correlation (or regression) coefficient between, say, the respondent's status and his father's education is an $n$th level highly mixed consequence of a *system* of factors. Trying to disentangle its meaning is simply a hopeless task. The key to a true explanation lies, here again, in the formalization of the underlying processes which are known to be at work.

Our contention is, in summary, that within, say, ten years, the development of a mathematical theory of mobility should have multiple important effects on social mobility research and perhaps even on all of sociology. But, it must also be realized that we are barely halfway along this road. Much further research is needed before we may actually speak of a mathematical theory of social mobility.

140

# Statistical Appendix*

In this appendix, we shall attempt to outline a general approach for the estimation of the parameters for the various models discussed in the text and for the comparison both among various models for a given set of data and among various sets of data for a given model. This general approach will make use of the likelihood function. No attempt will be made to draw absolute inferences, for example using tests of significance, from the data.

Before the data are available, it is possible to hypothesize one or more probability distributions ($M$) which might produce the data ($D$). The probability of observing the data for a given distribution (with all parameters known) will be $Pr\,(D;M)$. After collecting the data, $Pr\,(D;M)$ may be considered as a function of the unknown distribution (model) $M$ since $D$ is now known. Defining the likelihood function as being proportional to $Pr(D;M)$

$$L(M) = Pr\,(D;M) \qquad (5.1)**$$

We are interested in how probable a given model makes the data. Fortunately, in every case, there exists one model which makes the occurrence of the data most probable: that model which reproduces the data exactly. Thus, we use this model $\hat{M}$ as a basis for all comparisons, and define the relative likelihood function

$$R(M) = \frac{L(M)}{L(\hat{M})} \qquad (5.2)$$

---

* By J.K. Lindsey
** For the interpretation of $k$, see eqn. (5.13).

This function $R$ may vary between 0 and 1 and thus provides a metric for the comparison of all possible models.

Let us now consider some of the indices of the first chapter.

### 5.1. Social mobility measurement: measures without models

We shall consider the two principal indices of chapter 1: $M_Y$ and $M_B$.

The general likelihood function for the data considered in this chapter is derived from eqn. (1.1)

$$\hat{p}_{ij} = \frac{n_{ij}}{N} \tag{5.3}$$

Since $\Sigma_{i,j} p_{ij} = 1$, we may assume the distribution from which the data arises to be multinomial, so that the likelihood function is

$$L(P) = \prod_{i,j} p_{ij}{}^{n_{ij}} \tag{5.4}$$

Of course, the model which describes the data exactly is defined by eqn. (5.3). But, this model tells us very little about the data. We wish to find some relationship among the $p_{ij}$'s yielding an informative model which still allows the data to be reproduced fairly exactly as measured by the function $R$.

Consider now Yasuda's index

$$M_Y = \frac{N \min(n_{12}, n_{21})}{\min(n_{1.}, n_{.1}) \min(n_{2.}, n_{.2})} \tag{5.5}$$

from eqn. (1.19). If we consider the marginals as fixed, the parameter is

$$M_Y = \frac{N^2 p_{12}}{n_{1.} n_{.2}} \qquad (n_{12} < n_{21})$$

$$\tag{5.6}$$

$$= \frac{N^2 p_{21}}{n_{.1} n_{2.}} \qquad (n_{12} > n_{21})$$

Substituting this relationship and the constraints given by the marginals into the likelihood function (5.4), we obtain $L(M_Y)$

$$k_1(N-M_Y n_{.2})^{n_{11}} M_Y{}^{n_{12}} (n_{21} - n_{12} + M_Y n_{1.} n_{.2})^{n_{21}}$$

$$\times (N - M_Y n_{1.})^{n_{22}} \quad (n_{12} < n_{21})$$

$$k_2(N-M_Y n_{2.})^{n_{11}} M_Y{}^{n_{21}} (n_{12} - n_{21} + M_Y n_{.1} n_{2.})^{n_{12}}$$

$$\times (N - M_Y n_{.1})^{n_{22}} \quad (n_{12} > n_{21})$$

(5.7)

which is a function only of $M_Y$ with $k$ a constant. Hence, we obtain a new, more informative model which may be compared with the original model (5.3). The value of $M_Y$ which makes the data most probable (maximum likelihood estimate) *i.e.* which maximizes eqn. (5.7), is given by Yasuda's index (5.5). But, by varying the value of $M_Y$ in the likelihood function (5.7), we may determine the precision of the estimate. If a small change in $M_Y$ lowers considerably the probability of the observed data as measured by the likelihood function (5.7) substituted into eqn. (5.2), then the estimate is known with high precision.

The same analysis may be used with the index

$$M_B = \frac{\min(n_{12}, n_{21})}{\min(n_{11}, n_{22}) + \min(n_{12}, n_{21})}$$

(5.8)

from eqn. (1.37). Again with marginals fixed,

$$M_B = \frac{N p_{12}}{n_{1.}} \quad (n_{12} < n_{21}, n_{11} < n_{22})$$

$$= \frac{N p_{12}}{n_{.2}} \quad (n_{12} < n_{21}, n_{11} > n_{22})$$

$$= \frac{N p_{21}}{n_{.1}} \quad (n_{12} > n_{21}, n_{11} < n_{22})$$

$$= \frac{N p_{21}}{n_{2.}} \quad (n_{12} > n_{21}, n_{11} > n_{22})$$

(5.9)

143

In this case, we obtain four possible forms for the likelihood function, $L(M_B)$

$$k_1(1-M_B)^{n_{11}}M_B^{n_{12}}(n_{21}-n_{12}+M_Bn_{1.})^{n_{21}}(n_{2.}-M_Bn_{1.})^{n_{22}}$$

$$(n_{12}<n_{21},\, n_{11}<n_{22}) \qquad (5.10a)$$

$$k_2(1-M_B)^{n_{22}}M_B^{n_{12}}(n_{21}-n_{12}+M_Bn_{.2})^{n_{21}}(n_{1.}-M_Bn_{.2})^{n_{11}}$$

$$(n_{12}<n_{21},\, n_{11}>n_{22}) \qquad (5.10b)$$

$$k_3(1-M_B)^{n_{11}}M_B^{n_{21}}(n_{12}-n_{21}+M_Bn_{.1})^{n_{12}}(n_{.2}-M_Bn_{.1})^{n_{22}}$$

$$(n_{12}>n_{21},\, n_{11}<n_{22}) \qquad (5.10c)$$

$$k_4(1-M_B)^{n_{22}}M_B^{n_{21}}(n_{12}-n_{21}+M_Bn_{2.})^{n_{12}}(n_{.1}-M_Bn_{2.})^{n_{11}}$$

$$(n_{12}>n_{21},\, n_{11}>n_{22}) \qquad (5.10d)$$

with $k_i$ a constant. Again we obtain a new informative model with the maximum likelihood estimate of $M_B$ given by eqn. (5.8).

Further study of these two likelihood functions will help to clarify some of the problems encountered with these indices. Let us consider the data of Tables 5.1 and 5.2.

TABLE 5.1

| | | |
|---|---|---|
| 0 | 80 | 80 |
| 20 | 100 | 120 |
| 20 | 180 | 200 |

TABLE 5.2

| | | |
|---|---|---|
| 0 | 80 | 80 |
| 120 | 0 | 120 |
| 120 | 80 | 200 |

The two indices are, for Table 5.1, $M_Y = 5/3$ and $M_B = 1$, for Table 5.2 $M_Y = 5/2$ and $M_B = 1$. Hence, $M_Y$ indicates a difference between the tables whereas $M_B$ does not. But consider the likelihood function for $M_B$ for the two tables. For Table 5.1, $n_{12}>n_{21}$, $n_{11}<n_{22}$ so that eqn. (5.10c) is used, whereas for Table 5.2, $n_{12}<n_{21}$, $n_{11}=n_{22}$ so that eqn. (5.10a or b) is used. Hence, the index $M_B$ is actually different for the two tables. Thus, care must be taken in comparing the index ($M_B$ or $M_Y$) among tables if the tables do not all have likelihood functions of the same form.

144

We may consider the value of the index as indicating the magnitude of the mobility (*i.e.* the pure mobility) but not the type. As shown in Table 5.3, four types of mobility are distinguishable (considering status 1 as lower and 2 as upper). In Tables 5.4—5.7

TABLE 5.3

|  | $n_{12} < n_{21}$ | $n_{12} > n_{21}$ |
|---|---|---|
| $n_{11} < n_{22}$ | I  Downward mobility upper class stability (Table 5.4) | III  Upward mobility upper class stability (Table 5.6) |
| $n_{11} > n_{22}$ | II  Downward mobility lower class stability (Table 5.5) | IV  Upward mobility lower class stability (Table 5.7) |

are given examples of the four types of mobility. For all of the tables, $M_B = 0.5$ and $M_Y = 1.0$. But for the index $M_B$, each table corresponds to a different form of the likelihood function in eqn. (5.10). For the index $M_Y$, Tables 5.4 and 5.5 correspond to the same form of likelihood function in eqn. (5.7) and the remaining two tables to the other form. Thus, this index only distinguishes between upward and downward mobility and not as to which status group has the greater stability.

TABLE 5.4

| | | |
|---|---|---|
| 20 | 20 | 40 |
| 80 | 80 | 160 |
| 100 | 100 | 200 |

TABLE 5.5

| | | |
|---|---|---|
| 80 | 20 | 100 |
| 80 | 20 | 100 |
| 160 | 40 | 200 |

TABLE 5.6

| | | |
|---|---|---|
| 20 | 80 | 100 |
| 20 | 80 | 100 |
| 40 | 160 | 200 |

TABLE 5.7

| | | |
|---|---|---|
| 80 | 80 | 160 |
| 20 | 20 | 40 |
| 100 | 100 | 200 |

Suppose 200 sons are chosen in each of two countries, 100 from each of two classes and that the results are given by Tables 5.4

and 5.7. Then, considering only the magnitude of the index, the pure mobility of both tables is the same ($M_B = 0.5$) but, of course, the direction of the mobility is reversed between tables.

## 5.2. Measurements derived from mathematical models

Let us briefly review the notation used in Chapters 2, 3 and 4. Then, $N_t = [n_{(t)ij}]$ is the turnover mobility matrix from time $(t-1)$ to time $t$, with the corresponding transition matrix $R_t = [r_{(t)ij}]$ and $N^{(t)} = [n_{ij}{}^{(t)}]$ is the turnover mobility matrix from time 0 to time $t$, with the corresponding transition matrix $R^{(t)} = [r_{ij}{}^{(t)}] = \prod_t R_t$. For each $i$ in the transition matrices, $\sum_j r_{ij} = 1$.

For an individual in social stratum $i$, the probability of moving to stratum $j$ is given by $r_{ij}$, with $\sigma$ possible strata to which he may go. Then, each row of the matrix defines a multinomial distribution

$$\frac{(\sum_j n_j)!}{\prod_j n_{ij}!} \prod_j r_{ij}{}^{n_{ij}} \tag{5.11}$$

Since the rows are observed independently, the overall distribution of the matrix $N$ is given by

$$Pr(N; R) = \prod_i \frac{(\sum_j n_{ij})!}{\prod_j n_{ij}!} \prod_j r_{ij}{}^{n_{ij}} \tag{5.12}$$

After observing the mobility matrix, $N$, the corresponding likelihood function is

$$L(R) = \prod_i \prod_j r_{ij}{}^{n_{ij}} \tag{5.13}$$

since the multinomial coefficient $1/k$ [in the notation of eqn. (5.1)] does not contain $r_{ij}$.

The probability distribution (5.12) is relatively uninformative about the mechanism producing the observed mobility matrix. Thus, we introduce a mathematical model providing some relationship among the parameters $r_{ij}$. The first assumption, which is used in all of the models considered, is that the number of positions

146

available in the social strata to which the individuals go is fixed, *i.e.* the column totals of **N** are fixed at the observed values.

When a mathematical model is introduced, each $r_{ij}$ may be defined in terms of the parameters, **m**, of the model

$$r_{ij} = g_{ij}(\mathbf{m}) \tag{5.14}$$

Then, these values may be substituted into the likelihood function (5.13). The maximum likelihood estimate of **m** is that value which makes the probability of observing the given data greatest. Hence, we maximize the likelihood function. In order to do this, consider the log likelihood function

$$\log L(\mathbf{m}) = \sum_i \sum_j n_{ij} \log [g_{ij}(\mathbf{m})] \tag{5.15}$$

which is a monotone function of $L$ (*i.e.* will be maximum for the same **m**) and take partial derivatives with respect to each parameter of the vector **m**. Setting these derivatives equal to zero gives the likelihood equations which must be solved to obtain the maximum likelihood estimates.

Unfortunately, most of the models considered in this book yield nonlinear likelihood equations which must be solved by some iterative procedure. One general technique is Newton's method. Let $\mathbf{a}(\mathbf{m})$ be the vector of first derivatives of the log likelihood function (the likelihood equations with a given value of **m**), $\mathbf{A}(\mathbf{m})$ be the corresponding matrix of second derivatives, and $\mathbf{m}_0$ some initial estimate of the parameters. Then, successive estimates are given by

$$\mathbf{m}_{(i+1)}{}' = \mathbf{m}_i{}' - \mathbf{a}'(\mathbf{m}_i)\mathbf{A}^{-1}(\mathbf{m}_i) \tag{5.16}$$

until some convergence criterion is fulfilled.

If there are constraints on some of the parameters of **m**, *e.g.* $m_1 + m_2 + m_3 = k$, then additional parameters (Lagrange multipliers) are included in the estimation by adding terms of the form $\lambda(m_1 + m_2 + m_3 - k)$ to the log likelihood function (5.15) and considering the Lagrange multiplier, $\lambda$, as an additional parameter to be estimated. These additional parameters are only used to insure that the constraints are fulfilled, and may be ignored once the iterative process has converged to the maximum likelihood estimates.

Let us now consider the maximum likelihood estimates of $\mathbf{R}_t$ for given $t$ without introducing any further assumptions. With the Lagrange multipliers, the log likelihood function becomes

$$\sum_i [\sum_j n_{(t)ij} \log(r_{(t)ij}) + \lambda_i (\sum_j r_{(t)ij} - 1)] \qquad (5.17)$$

Then, the likelihood equations are

$$\frac{\partial}{\partial r_{(t)ij}} : \frac{n_{(t)ij}}{\hat{r}_{(t)ij}} + \hat{\lambda}_i = 0 \qquad (i = 1, ..., \sigma; \; j = 1, ..., \sigma)$$

$$\qquad (5.18)$$

$$\frac{\partial}{\partial \lambda_i} : \sum_j \hat{r}_{(t)ij} - 1 = 0 \qquad (i = 1, ..., \sigma)$$

These equations are linear and may easily be solved to give $\hat{r}_{(t)ij} = n_{(t)ij}/n_{(t)i}$. Then, the maximized log likelihood function is

$$\log L(\hat{\mathbf{R}}_t) = \sum_i \sum_j n_{(t)ij} \log(n_{(t)ij}/\sum_k n_{(t)ik}) \qquad (5.19)$$

When a mathematical model is introduced, the maximum value of the likelihood function attainable is less than that given by eqn. (5.19). Thus, this equation provides a basis with which any model may be compared to determine how good is the fit of the model. Using eqn. (5.2), the measure of fit is given by the log relative likelihood

$$\log R(\mathbf{R}_t) = \sum_i \sum_j n_{(t)ij} [\log \mathbf{r}_{(t)ij} - \log(n_{(t)ij}/\sum_k n_{(t)ik})] \quad (5.20)$$

with $\mathbf{R}_t$ given by eqn. (5.14).

*Markov chains*

For a Markov chain, $\mathbf{R}_t = \mathbf{R}$ for all $t$ yielding $\mathbf{R}^{(t)} = \mathbf{R}^t$. If mobility matrices $\mathbf{N}_t$ are available for several successive time periods, the likelihood function is given by

$$\log L(\mathbf{R}) = \sum_t \sum_i \sum_j n_{(t)ij} \log(r_{ij}) \qquad (5.21)$$

with maximum likelihood estimates

$$\hat{r}_{ij} = \sum_t n_{(t)ij}/\sum_t n_{(t)i} \qquad (5.22)$$

To determine how well this model fits for each individual mobility

148

matrix, the estimates of eqn. (5.22) are substituted into the relative likelihood function (5.20)

$$\log R(\mathbf{R}) = \sum_i \sum_j n_{(t)ij} [\log(\sum_k n_{(k)ij} / \sum_k n_{(k)i})$$

$$- \log(n_{(t)ij} / \sum_k n_{(t)ik})] \qquad (5.23)$$

for each value of $t$. The function $R$ may vary between 0 and 1 with larger values indicating a better fit.

Of course, if a mobility matrix is available for only one time period, the estimates (5.22) reduce to those derived from the likelihood equations (5.18).

*White's intergenerational mover—stayer model*

For White's model using the assumption of perfect mobility, the relationship among the elements of the transition matrix may be derived from eqn. (2.59)

$$r_{ii} = \frac{m_{(0)i}(m_{(0)i} - n_{(0)i} + n_{(1)i})}{Mn_{(0)i}} + \frac{n_{(0)i} - m_{(0)i}}{n_{(0)i}}$$

$$(5.24)$$

$$r_{ij} = \frac{m_{(0)i}(m_{(0)j} - n_{(0)j} + n_{(i)j})}{Mn_{(0)i}} \qquad (i \neq j)$$

with vector of parameters, $\mathbf{m}_{(0)}$ and $M$ to be estimated. These relationships yield the log likelihood function

$$\log L(\mathbf{m}_{(0)}) = \sum_i n_{ii} \log \frac{m_{(0)i}(m_{(0)i} - n_{(0)i} + n_{(1)i})}{Mn_{(0)i}} + \frac{n_{(0)i} - m_{(0)i}}{n_{(0)i}}$$

$$+ \sum \sum_{i \neq j} n_{ij} \log \frac{m_{(0)i}(m_{(0)j} - n_{(0)j} + n_{(1)j})}{Mn_{(0)i}} \qquad (5.25)$$

with the constraint that $\Sigma_i m_{(0)i} = M$. Then, with Lagrange multiplier, $\lambda$, the likelihood equations to be solved are

$$\frac{n_{ij}(2\hat{m}_{(0)i} - n_{(0)i} + n_{(1)i} - \hat{M}}{\hat{m}_{(0)i}(\hat{m}_{(0)i} - n_{(0)i} + n_{(1)i}) + \hat{M}(n_{(0)i} - \hat{m}_{(0)i})}$$

$$+ \sum_{j \neq i} n_{ij} \left( \frac{1}{\hat{m}_{(0)i}} + \frac{1}{\hat{m}_{(0)i} - n_{(0)i} + n_{(1)i}} \right) + \hat{\lambda} = 0 \qquad (i = 1, ..., \sigma)$$

$$\sum_i \frac{-n_{ii}\hat{m}_{(0)i}(\hat{m}_{(0)i} - n_{(0)i} + n_{(1)i})}{\hat{M}\hat{m}_{(0)i}(\hat{m}_{(0)i} - n_{(0)i} + n_{(1)i}) + \hat{M}^2(n_{(0)i} - \hat{m}_{(0)i})}$$

$$- \sum_{i \neq j} \sum \frac{n_{ij}}{\hat{M}} - \hat{\lambda} = 0$$

$$\sum_i \hat{m}_{(0)i} - \hat{M} = 0 \qquad\qquad\qquad (5.26)$$

When these non-linear equations have been solved to give numerical estimates of the parameters, the relationships of eqn. (5.24) may be used in the relative likelihood function (5.20) to determine how well this model fits the data.

*Goodman's mover—stayer model*
As described in the text, the estimates for Goodman's model may be obtained directly yielding

$$\hat{r}_{ii} = n_{ii}/n_{(0)i}$$

$$\hat{r}_{ij} = (n_{(0)i} - n_{ii})(n_{(1)j} - n_{jj})/[(N - \sum_k n_{kk})n_{(0)i}] \quad (i \neq j) \ (5.27)$$

since

$$\hat{m}_{(0)i} = n_{(0)i} - n_{ii}, \ \hat{m}_{(1)j} = n_{(1)j} - n_{jj}$$

and

$$\hat{M} = N - \sum_i n_{ii}$$

The relationships of eqn. (5.27) are then used in the relative likelihood to determine the fit, and for comparison with other models such as White's.

*The Type 3 model*
We shall consider this model in the case where $g > 2$ since this adds no further complications to the case where $g = 2$. From eqns. (2.70) and (2.71), the relationship among the $r_{ij}$'s is given by

$$r_{ij} = \sum_k \frac{m_{(0)i}{}^k m_{(1)j}{}^k}{M_k n_{(0)j}} \qquad (5.28)$$

and the log likelihood function by

$$\log L(\mathbf{m}_{(0)}, \mathbf{m}_{(1)}, \mathbf{M}) = \sum_i \sum_j n_{ij} \log \left[ \sum_k \frac{m_{(0)i}{}^k m_{(1)j}{}^k}{M_k n_{(0)i}} \right] \qquad (5.29)$$

with the following constraints

$$\sum_k m_{(0)i}{}^k = n_{(0)i}$$

$$\sum_k m_{(1)j}{}^k = n_{(1)j}$$

$$\sum_k m_{(0)i}{}^k = M_k = \sum_j m_{(1)j}{}^k$$

$$\sum_k M_k = N$$

Theoretically, all of the constraints may be substituted into the likelihood function but this complicates greatly the first and second derivatives required.

Thus some of the constraints will be substituted directly into the likelihood function while others will require Lagrange multipliers. Then, the likelihood equations are

$$\frac{\sum_j n_{ij} \left( \dfrac{\hat{m}_{(i)j}{}^l}{\hat{M}_l} - \dfrac{\hat{m}_{(i)j}{}^g}{\hat{M}_g} \right)}{\sum_k \left( \dfrac{\hat{m}_{(0)i}{}^k \hat{m}_{(i)j}{}^k}{\hat{M}_k} \right)} + \beta_l = 0 \qquad \begin{aligned} & i = 1, ..., \sigma \\ & l = 1, ..., (g-1) \end{aligned}$$

$$\sum_i \left\{ \frac{n_{ij} \left( \dfrac{\hat{m}_{(0)i}{}^l}{\hat{M}_l} - \dfrac{\hat{m}_{(0)i}{}^g}{\hat{M}_g} \right)}{\sum_k \left( \dfrac{\hat{m}_{(0)i}{}^k \hat{m}_{(i)j}{}^k}{\hat{M}_k} \right)} - \sum_s \frac{n_{is} \left( \dfrac{\hat{m}_{(0)i}{}^l \hat{m}_{(1)s}{}^l}{\hat{M}_l{}^2} - \dfrac{\hat{m}_{(0)i}{}^g \hat{m}_{(1)s}{}^g}{\hat{M}_g{}^2} \right)}{\sum_k \left( \dfrac{\hat{m}_{(0)i}{}^k \hat{m}_{(1)s}{}^k}{\hat{M}_k} \right)} \right\}$$

$$-\beta_l = 0 \qquad\qquad j = 1, \ldots, \sigma$$
$$l = 1, \ldots, (g-1)$$

where

$$\hat{M}_l = \sum_j \hat{m}_{(i)j}{}^k, \quad \hat{m}_{(0)i}{}^g = n_{(0)i} - \sum_{l=1}^{(g-1)} \hat{m}_{(0)j}{}^l \, ,$$

and

$$\hat{m}_{(1)j}{}^g = n_{(1)j} - \sum_{i=1}^{(g-1)} \hat{m}_{(1)j}{}^l$$

$$\sum_i (\hat{m}_{(0)i}{}^l - \hat{m}_{(i)j}{}^l = 0 \qquad\qquad (l = 1, \ldots, (g-1)) \qquad (5.30)$$

with Lagrange multipliers $\beta_l$, where $\hat{M}_l$ (all $l$), $\hat{m}_{(0)i}{}^g$ (all $i$), and $\hat{m}_{(1)j}{}^g$ (all $j$) are given by the constraints above.

The $\hat{m}_{(0)\sigma}{}^k$ are given by the relationship

$$\hat{m}_{(0)\sigma}{}^k = \hat{M}_k - \sum_{i=1}^{(\sigma-1)} \hat{m}_{(0)i}{}^k \qquad\qquad (5.31)$$

After solving these non-linear likelihood equations for the maximum likelihood estimates of $m_{(0)}$, $m_{(1)}$, and $M$, we use the same procedure as above to determine goodness of fit, and for comparison with other models.

## 5.3. Theories without intervening variables

All of the models so far considered have been intergenerational with the turnover mobility matrix $\mathbf{N}_t$ available for only one time period. For the intragenerational models considered in this appendix, with observations available for a number of time periods, we may wish to determine the goodness of fit over several time periods (i.e. of $\mathbf{R}^{(t)}$ to $\mathbf{N}^{(t)}$) as well as the individual fits at each time period, (i.e. of $\mathbf{R}_t$ to $\mathbf{N}_t$ for each $t$). This is done in exactly the same way as previously with the individual $\mathbf{R}_t$ using the relative likelihood (5.20) but replacing $\mathbf{R}_t$ and $\mathbf{N}_t$ by $\mathbf{R}^{(t)}$ and $\mathbf{N}^{(t)}$ respectively. Thus, we obtain, for example, an exact measure of the poor fit found by Blumen for $\mathbf{R}^{(4)}$ and $\mathbf{R}^{(11)}$ of the original mover — stayer model.

After a model has been found to explain a given set of data

well, we may wish to see if the same model (with the same parameter estimates) will explain satisfactorily other sets of data. Again, the relative likelihood function (5.20) provides a measure of fit. The maximum likelihood estimates from the first set of data are used with the second set of data in this function to obtain an absolute measure of fit (*i.e.* as compared with the best possible for the second set of data). This relative likelihood may be compared with that using the maximum likelihood estimates from the second set to obtain a relative measure of fit (*i.e.* comparing how well the two sets of estimates explain the second set of data). These procedures are, of course, applicable to the intergenerational models of Chapter 2 as well as to those to be discussed below.

*The original mover—stayer model using the equilibrium matrix*

For intragenerational data with more than one mobility matrix available, we assume that for $t = k$ sufficiently large an equilibrium matrix is reached, as given by eqn. (3.1). Then, the maximum likelihood estimates are derived using the relationship of eqns. (3.5)

$$r_{ii}^{(k)} = s_i + (1 - s_i)m_i{}^*$$

$$r_{ij}^{(k)} = (1 - s_i)m_j{}^*$$

(5.32)

In this case, we use the mobility matrix $\mathbf{N}^{(k)}$ from time 0 to $k$ to estimate the parameters, **s** and **m***. Then the log likelihood function is

$$\log L(\mathbf{s}, \mathbf{m}^*) = \sum_i n_{ii}{}^{(k)} \log[(1 - s_i)m_i{}^* + s_i]$$

$$+ \sum\sum_{i \ne j} n_{ij}{}^{(k)} \log[(1 - s_i)m_j{}^*]$$

(5.33)

with the constraint that $\Sigma m_i{}^* = 1$. Then, with Lagrange multiplier, $\lambda$, the likelihood equations are

$$\frac{n_{ii}{}^{(k)}(1 - \hat{m}_i{}^*)}{(1 - \hat{s}_i)\hat{m}_i{}^* + \hat{s}_i} - \frac{\sum\limits_{j \ne i} n_{ij}{}^{(k)}}{1 - \hat{s}_i} = 0 \qquad (i = 1, \dots, \sigma)$$

$$\frac{n_{ii}{}^{(k)}(1 - \hat{s}_i)}{(1 - \hat{s}_i)\hat{m}_i{}^* + \hat{s}_i} + \frac{\sum\limits_{j \ne i} n_{ji}{}^{(k)}}{\hat{m}_i{}^*} + \lambda = 0 \qquad (i = 1, \dots, \sigma)$$

(5.34)

153

$$\sum_i \hat{m}_i{}^* = 1$$

The elements of the transition matrix **M** for the movers remain to be estimated. As stated in the text, we use eqn. (3.2a) in this estimation

$$\hat{\mathbf{M}} = (\mathbf{I} - \hat{\mathbf{S}})^{-1}(\hat{\mathbf{R}}^{(1)} - \hat{\mathbf{S}}) \tag{5.35}$$

although this ignores the information about **M** in the other mobility matrices between times 1 and $k$. For any given time period, the transition matrix is given by

$$\mathbf{R}_t = [\mathbf{S} + (\mathbf{I} - \mathbf{S})\mathbf{M}^{(t-1)}]^{-1}[\mathbf{S} + (\mathbf{I} - \mathbf{S})\mathbf{M}^t] \tag{5.36}$$

By inserting the estimates, $\hat{\mathbf{S}}$ and $\hat{\mathbf{M}}$, and using the relative likelihood function (5.20), the fit of the model at each quarter may be determined. Likewise, using the relationships of eqn. (3.2), the fit of the model over the period 0 to $t$ may be determined.

*Collective history model*

In the collective history model, we wish to estimate the rates of change of the elements of the transition matrix, $\mathbf{R}_t$. At a given time period, the elements of the matrix $\mathbf{R}_t$ are defined in terms of the elements of the previous matrix $\mathbf{R}_{t-1}$ and of the matrix **X**

$$r_{(t)ii} = \frac{r_{(t-1)ii}(1 + x_i)}{1 + x_i r_{(t-1)ii}}$$

$$\tag{5.37}$$

$$r_{(t)ij} = \frac{r_{(t-1)ij}}{1 + x_i r_{(t-1)ii}} \qquad (i \neq j)$$

Then, substituting the observed values of the mobility matrix for the elements of the matrix $\mathbf{R}_{(t-1)}$, the log likelihood function for estimation of **X** is

$$\log L(\mathbf{X}) = \sum_t \left\{ \sum_i n_{(t)ii} \log[n_{(t-1)ii}(1 + x_i)] \right.$$

$$+ \sum_{i \neq j}\sum n_{(t)ij} \log(n_{(t-1)ij})$$

$$\left. - \sum_i\sum_j n_{(t)ij} \log(n_{(t-1)i} + n_{(t-1)ii}x_i) \right\} \tag{5.38}$$

from which the likelihood equations are derived

$$\sum_i \left\{ \frac{n_{(t)ii}}{1+\hat{x}_i} - \frac{n_{(t)i}\,n_{(t-1)ii}}{n_{(t-1)i} + n_{(t-1)ii}\hat{x}_i} \right\} = 0 \qquad (i = 1, ..., \sigma) \qquad (5.39)$$

When these equations have been solved for the estimates $\hat{x}_i$, the relationships of eqn. (5.37) may be used with the relative likelihood function (5.20) to determine how well the model fits at each time interval. Note that, in this case, we start with the initial time interval using the observed mobility matrix from the beginning to the end of the first quarter to calculate the transition matrix for the next quarter. But, thereafter we use the previous predicted transition matrix to calculate the next.

TABLE 5.8

| 0 | | | | $n_{(0)1}$ | $n_{(0)2}$ | | | $n_{(0)1}$ |
|---|---|---|---|---|---|---|---|---|
| | | | | | $\mathbf{R}(0)$ | | | $n_{(0)2}$ |
| 1 | | | $n_{(1)11}^0$ | | $n_{(1)12}^0$ | | | $n_{(1)1}$ |
| | | | $n_{(1)22}^0$ | | $n_{(1)21}^0$ | | | $n_{(1)2}$ |
| | | $\mathbf{R}(1)$ | | $\mathbf{R}(0)$ | | | | |
| 2 | | $n_{(2)11}^1$ | $n_{(2)12}^1$ | $n_{(2)11}^0$ | $n_{(2)12}^0$ | | | $n_{(2)1}$ |
| | | $n_{(2)22}^1$ | $n_{(2)21}^1$ | $n_{(2)22}^0$ | $n_{(2)21}^0$ | | | $n_{(2)2}$ |
| | $\mathbf{R}(2)$ | | $\mathbf{R}(1)$ | | $\mathbf{R}(0)$ | | | |
| 3 | $n_{(3)11}^2$ | $n_{(3)12}^2$ $n_{(3)11}^1$ | $n_{(3)12}^1$ $n_{(3)11}^0$ | $n_{(3)12}^0$ $n_{(3)1}$ | | | | |
| | $n_{(3)22}^2$ | $n_{(3)21}^2$ $n_{(3)22}^1$ | $n_{(3)21}^1$ $n_{(3)22}^0$ | $n_{(3)21}^0$ $n_{(3)2}$ | | | | |
| | $\mathbf{R}(3)$ | $\mathbf{R}(2)$ | | $\mathbf{R}(1)$ | $\mathbf{R}(0)$ | | | |

*Cornell Mobility Model with axiom B*

Without introducing additional assumptions, the transition matrices for the sub-populations may be estimated as follows. Since we know the individual histories at each quarter, the population may be split into sub-populations having stayed a given number of times. At quarter $t$, let $n_{(t)ij}{}^k$ be the number going from category $i$ to $j$ who have previously stayed $k$ times *i.e.* the individual $n_{(t)ii}{}^k$ are now staying for the $(k+1)$th time. Then, the population divides as in Table 5.8 for two classes.

Since all of the values $n_{(t)ii}{}^k$ have been observed, they may be used to estimate the corresponding $\mathbf{R}(k)$ in the same way as above with eqn. (5.18). Thus, the maximum likelihood estimates are

$$\hat{r}_{ij}(k) = \sum_{t=(k+1)}^{s} n_{(t)ij}{}^k \Big/ \sum_{t=(k+1)}^{s} n_{(t)i}{}^k \qquad (5.40)$$

where data up to quarter $s$ are available. The elements of the transition matrix of the whole population are given by

$$r_{(t)ij} = \frac{\displaystyle\sum_{k=0}^{(t-1)} r_{ij}(k) n_{(t)ij}{}^k}{n_{(t)i}} \qquad (5.41)$$

which may be used with the maximum likelihood estimates of eqn. (5.40) and the relative likelihood function (5.20) to determine goodness of fit of the model.

## 5.4. Discussion

One may ask why the multinomial distribution is always used for estimation of parameters when it is sometimes possible to calculate least squares estimates of the parameters by solving linear equations. In most of the models considered, the least squares equations will also be non-linear. In addition, the least squares estimation introduces the assumption of the normal distribution. This may be illustrated in a simple case. Suppose we have two possible categories and obtain two sets of observations giving proportions 2/7 and 20/21. Then, the estimate of the combined proportion using the method outlined above is $(2 + 20)/(7 + 21) = 22/28 = 11/14$ whereas the least squares (normal distribution maximum likelihood) estimate is $(2/7 + 20/21)/2 = (26/21)/2 = 13/21$. Thus, the least squares estimate does not take into account the fact that three times as many observations are available in the second set and does not weight accordingly.

The relationship of the measure of fit of a model given by $R$ of eqns. (5.2) and (5.20) to that given by the classical asymptotic $\chi^2$ goodness of fit test for such tables is also worth mentioning. From the value of $R$ obtained for a given model, an asymptotic likelihood ratio test is derived since $-2 \log R$ is asymptotically distributed as a Chi-square with degrees of freedom equal to the difference in number of parameters estimated in the two likelihood functions of the ratio (see eqn. (5.2)), *i.e.* with the same number of degrees of freedom as for the classical goodness of fit test. It should be noted that both of these tests introduce an additional assumption of normality (from which the distribution is derived) and that both hold only asymptotically, *i.e.* when the total number, $N$, of observations in the table is very large. Thus, the two tests may give different results for a given observed table unless $N$ is very large, since the asymptotic assumption will not have been fulfilled. In the previously outlined procedures, we have avoided this additional assumption of normality in making inferences and have been content with comparing the plausibility of various models using the relative likelihood ratio $R$.

## Bibliography for Appendix

Barnard, J.A., Jenkins, G.M. and Winston, C.B. (1962). "Likelihood Inference and Time Series", *J. Roy. Statistical Soc.*, A125, 321—372.

Fisher, R.A. (1959). *Statistical Methods and Scientific Inference*, 178 pp. Edinburgh: Oliver and Boyd.

Sprott, D.A. and Kalbfleisch, J.G. (1965). "Use of the Likelihood Function in Inference", *Psychological Bull. 64*, 15—22.

Sprott, D.A. and Kalbfleisch, J.G. (1969). "Examples of Likelihoods and Comparison with Point Estimates and Large Sample Approximations", *J. Amer. Statistical Assoc. 64*, 468—484.

# Bibliography

Anderson, C.A. (1961). "A Skeptical Note on Education and Mobility," *Amer. J. Sociol.* 66 (1), 560—570.

Bartlett, M.S. (1955). *An Introduction to Stochastic Processes*. New York: Cambridge University Press.

Barclay, G.W. (1958). *Techniques of Population Analysis*. New York: Wiley.

Bartholomew, D.J. (1967). *Stochastic Models for Social Processes*. New York: Wiley.

Bertaux, D. (1969). "Sur l'analyse des Tables de Mobilité Sociale," *Rev. Franc. Sociol.* 10(4), 448—490.

Bertaux, D. (1971). "Nouvelles Perspectives sur la Mobilité Sociale en France," *Quality and Quantity* 5(1), 87—130.

Billewicz, W.Z. (1955). "Some Remarks on the Measurement of Social Mobility," *Population Studies* 9, 96—100.

Blau, P. and O.D. Duncan (1967). *The American Occupational Structure*. New York: Wiley.

Blumen, I., M. Kogan and P.J. McCarthy (1955). "The Industrial Mobility of Labor as a Probability Process," *Cornell Studies in Industrial and Labor Relations VI.*

Blumen, I., M. Kogan and P.J. McCarthy (1966). "Probability Models for Mobility," in Lazarsfeld, P. and Henry, M. eds., *Readings in Mathematical Social Science*, pp.318—334. Chicago: Science Research Associates.

Boudon, R. (1970). "Essai sur la Mobilité Sociale en Utopie," *Quality and Quantity* 4(2), 213—242.

Boudon, R. (1971a). "Eléments pour une Théorie Formelle de la Mobilité Sociale," *Quality and Quantity* 5(1), 39—85.

Boudon, R. (1971b). "Why Comparative Mobility Studies often Lead to so Confusing Results: a Methodological Case Study and an Exercise in Theory Building," paper prepared for the *Symposium on Highly Industrialized Societies*. Bellagio: International Social Sciences Council.

Boudon, R. (1972). "A Note on Social Inequality and Immobility Measurement," *Quality and Quantity* 6 (1), 17—35.

Boudon, R. (1973a). "Note on a Model for the Analysis of Mobility Tables," *Social Science Information*, (in the press).

Boudon, R. (1973b). *Education, Opportunity, and Social Inequality. Changing Prospects in Western Society.* New York: Wiley. In the press.

Capecchi, V. (1967). "Problèmes Méthodologiques dans la Mesure de la Mobilité Sociale," *Arch. Européennes Sociol.* 8 (12), 285—318.

Carlsson, G. (1958). *Social Mobility and Class Structure. Lund Studies in Sociology.* Lund: C.W.K. Gleerup.

Carlsson, G. and K. Karlsson (1970). "Age, Cohorts and the Generation of Generations," *Amer. Sociol. Rev.* 35 (4), 710—717.

Centers, R. (1949). "Education and Occupational Mobility," *Amer. Sociol. Rev.* 14, 143—144.

Coleman, J.S. (1964). *Introduction to Mathematical Sociology.* Glencoe; the Free Press of Glencoe.

Coleman, J.S. (1968). "Demand and Supply Considerations in Mobility," presented to the *Cornell Conference in Human Mobility, Ithaca.*

Coleman, J.S. (1971). *A Flow Model for Occupational Structures.* Baltimore: Johns Hopkins University. (Mimeographed).

Courgeau, D. (1970). *Les Champs Migratoires en France.* Paris: Presses Universitaires de France.

Deming, W.E. (1943). *Statistical Adjustment of Data.* New York: Dover. (Reprinted 1964).

Dodd, S.C. (1950). "The Interactance Hypothesis: A Gravity Model Fitting Physical Masses and Human Groups," *Amer. Sociol. Rev.* 15 (2), 245—256.

Duncan, O.D. (1966). "Methodological Issues in the Analysis of Social Mobility," in Smelser, N. and Lipset. S. eds., *Social Structures and Mobility in Economic Development*, pp.51—97. Chicago: Aldine.

Duncan, O.D. and P.N. Hauser (1959). "An Inventory and Appraisal," *The Study of Populations* 864 pp. Chicago: University of Chicago Press.

Duncan, O.D. and N.R. Hodge (1963). "Educational and Occupational Mobility: a Regression Analysis," *Amer. J. Sociol.* 68, 629—644.

Durbin, J. (1955). "Appendix Note on a Statistical Question Raised in the Preceding Paper," *Population Studies*, 101.

Feller, W. (1950, 1965). *An Introduction to Probability Theory and its Applications.* Vol. I, Vol. II. New York: Wiley.

Gabor, D. and A. Gabor (1954). "An Essay on Mathematical Theory of Freedom," *J. Roy. Statistical Soc., A* 117, 31—72.

Gabor, A. (1955). "The Concept of Statistical Freedom and its Applications to Social Mobility," *Population Studies* 9, 82—95.

Gabor, D. and A. Gabor (1958). "L'Entropie comme Mesure de la Liberté Sociale et Économique," *Cahiers de l'I.S.E.A. II*, 13—26.

Ginsberg, R.B. (1971). "Semi-Markov Processes and Mobility," *J. Mathematical Sociol.* 1 (2), 233—262.

Girod, R. (1971). *Mobilité Sociale.* Genève: Droz.

Glass, D.V. (1954). *Social Mobility in Britain.* London: Routledge and Kegan Paul.

Goodman, L. (1961). "Statistical Methods for a Mover—Stayer Model," *J. Amer. Statistical Assoc.* 56, 841—868.

Goodman, L. (1965). "On the Statistical Analysis of Mobility Tables," *Amer. J. Sociol.* 70, 564—585.

159

Goodman, L. (1968). "The Analysis of Cross Classified Data: Independence, Quasi Independence and Interactions in Contingency Tables with or without Missing Entries," *J. Amer. Statistical Assoc.* 68, 1091—1131.

Goodman, L. (1969a). "How to Ransack Social Mobility Tables and Other Kinds of Cross Classification Tables," *Amer. J. Sociol.* 75 (1), 1—40.

Goodman, L. (1969b). "On the Measurement of Social Mobility: an Index of Status Persistence," *Amer. Sociol. Rev.* 34 (6), 831—850.

Hajnal, J. (1956). "The Ergodic Properties of Non-Homogeneous Finite Markov Chains," *Proc. Cambridge Phil. Soc.* 52, 67—77.

Hajnal, J. (1958). "Weak Ergodicity in Non-Homogeneous Markov Chains," *Proc. Cambridge Phil. Soc.* 54, 233—246.

Hall, J.R. "Rambrishna Mukerjee, a Note on the Analysis of Data on Social Mobility," in Glass, D.V. ed., *Social Mobility in Britain*, 218—220.

Henry, N.W. (1971). "The Retention Model: A Markov Chain with Variable Transition Probabilities," *J. Amer. Statistical Assoc.* 66, 264—267.

Henry, N.W., R. McGinnis and H.W. Tegmeyer (1971). "A Finite Model of Mobility," *J. Mathematical Sociol.* 1 (1), 107—118.

Hill, J.M.M. (1951). "A Consideration of Labor Turnover as the Resultant of a Quasi Stationary Process," *Human Relations* 4, 255—264.

Hodge, R.W. (1966). "Occupational Mobility as a Probability Process," *Demography* 3, 19—34.

Jackson, E.F. and H.J. Crockett, Jr. (1964). "Occupational Mobility in the United States: a Point Estimate and Trend Comparison," *Amer. Sociol. Rev.* 29(1), 5—15.

Kahl, A. (1957). *The American Class Structure.* New York: Rinehart.

Karlin, S. (1968). *A First Course in Stochastic Processes.* New York: Academic Press.

Kemeny, J.G., J.L. Snell and G.L. Thompson (1957). *Finite Mathematics.* Englewood Cliffs: Prentice Hall.

Kemeny, J.G. and J.L. Snell (1960). *Finite Markov Chains.* Princeton: van Nostrand.

Keyfitz, N. (1964). "Matrix Multiplication as a Technique of Population Analysis." *Milbank Memorial Fund Quarterly*, 42, 68—84.

Keyfitz, N. (1968). *Introduction to the Mathematics of Population.* Reading (Mass): Addison Wesley.

Lazarsfeld, P. and N. Henry (1966). *Readings in Mathematical Sociology.* Chicago: Science Research Associates.

Lazarsfeld, P. and N. Henry (1968). *Latent Structure Analysis.* Boston: Houghton-Mifflin.

Levine, J.H. (1967). *Measurement in the Study of Intergenerational Status Mobility* (Ph. D. Thesis). Cambridge: Harvard University, Department of Social Relations.

Lipset, S.M. and R. Bendix (1960). *Social Mobility in Industrial Societies.* Berkeley: the University of California Press.

Livi, L. (1950). "Sur la Mesure de la Mobilité Sociale," *Population* VI, 65—76.

Matras, J. (1960). "Comparison of Intergenerational Occupational Mobility Patterns: an Application to the Formal Theory of Social Mobility," *Population Studies* 14, 163—169.

*look at this [ see sect. 4.2 this book ].*

*— a 1960*

Matras, J. (1961). "Differential Fertility, Intergenerational Occupational Mobility and Change in the Occupational Distribution: some Elementary Interrelationships," *Population Studies* 15, 187—197.

Matras, J. (1966). "Social Mobility and Social Structure: some Insights from the Linear Model," paper presented at the *6th World Congress of Sociology, Evian, France. Amer. Sociol. Rev.* 32 (1967) 608—614.

Matras, J. (1967). "Set up a Matrix of Social Mobility," *Amer. Sociol. Rev.,* 608—614.

Mayer, T.F. (1967). "Birth and Death Process Models of Social Mobility," *Michigan Studies in Mathematical Sociology*, Vol. 2, University of Michigan.

Mayer, T.F. (1968). "Age and Mobility: Two Approaches to the Problem of Non-Stationary," *Michigan Studies in Mathematical Sociology*, Vol. 6, University of Michigan.

McFarland, D.D. (1968). "An Extension of Conjoint Measurement to Test the Theory of Quasi Perfect Mobility," *Michigan Studies in Mathematical Sociology*, Vol. 3, University of Michigan.

McFarland, D.D. (1969). "Measuring the Permeability of Occupational Structures," *Amer. J. Sociol.* 75, 41—61.

McFarland, D.D. (1970). "Intragenerational Social Mobility as a Markov Process: Including a Time Stationary Markovian Model that Explains Observed Declines in Mobility Rates," *Amer. Sociol. Rev.* 35 (3), 463—475.

McGinnis, R. (1968). "A Stochastic Model of Social Mobility," *Amer. Sociol. Rev.* 33 (5), 712—722.

Miller, S.M. (1960). "Comparative Social Mobility," *Current Sociol.* IX, 1—89.

Mosteller, F. (1968). "Association and Estimation in Contingency Tables," *J. Amer. Statistical Assoc.* 63, 1—28.

O.E.C.D. (1970). *Structures Professionnelles et Educatives et Niveaux de Développement Économique.* Paris: O.E.C.D. *look at this!*

Prais, S.J. (1955a). "The Formal Theory of Social Mobility," *Population Studies* 9, 72—81.

Prais, S.J. (1955b). "Measuring Social Mobility," *J. Roy. Statistical Assoc., A* 118, 56—66.

Pullum, T.W. (1964). The Theoretical Implications of Quasi Perfect Mobility. (unpublished manuscript). Chicago: the University of Chicago.

Pullum, T.W. (1968). Occupational Mobility as a Branching Process. (unpublished manuscript). Chicago: the University of Chicago.

Pullum, T.W. (1970). "What Can Mathematical Models Tell us about Occupational Mobility?", *Sociol. Inquiry* 40 (2), 258—280.

Rice, A.K. and J.M. Hill (1950). "The Representation of Labour Turnover as a Social Process," *Human Relations* 3, 349—381.

Rogoff, N. (1953). *Recent Trends in Occupational Mobility.* Glencoe: the Free Press of Glencoe.

Smelser, N. and S. Lipset (1966). *Social Structure and Mobility in Economic Development.* Chicago: Aldine.

Sorokin, P. (1927). *Social Mobility.* New edition, *Social and Cultural Mobility.* Glencoe: The Free Press of Glencoe.

Stouffer, S.A. (1962). *Social Research to Test Ideas.* Glencoe: the Free Press of Glencoe.

Svalastoga, K. (1959). *Prestige, Class and Mobility*. Copenhagen: Gyldendal.

Svalastoga, K. (1965). "Social Mobility: the Western European Model," *Acta Sociol.* IX, 175—182.

Tugnault, Y. (1970). "Méthode d'Analyse d'un Tableau Origine—Destination de Migrations," *Population* 25.

Tumin, M. and S.A. Feldman (1957). "Theory and Measurement of Occupational Mobility," *Amer. Sociol. Rev.* 22 (3), 281—288.

Westoff, Ch. F. (1953). "The Changing Focus of Differential Fertility Research; the Social Mobility Hypothesis," *Milbank Memorial Fund Quarterly* 31. Reprinted in Spengler, J.J. and Duncan, O.D., eds., *Population Theory and Policy*. Glencoe: the Free Press of Glencoe, 1956, pp.400—409.

White, H. (1963). "Causes and Effect in Social Mobility Tables," *Behavioral Sciences* 8, 14—27.

White, H. (1970a). *Chains of Opportunity; System Models of Mobility in Organizations*. Cambridge: Harvard University Press.

White, H. (1970b). "Stayers and Movers," *Amer. J. Sociol.* 76 (2) 307—324.

Yasuda, S. (1964). "A Methodological Inquiry into Social Mobility," *Amer. Sociol. Rev.* 29 (1), 16—23.

162

# Analytical Index

164

? general ?

165

166

168